Cambridge Elements

Elements in Language Teaching
edited by
Heath Rose
University of Oxford
Jim McKinley
University College London

METACOGNITION IN LANGUAGE TEACHING

Mark Feng Teng
Macao Polytechnic University

Shaftesbury Road, Cambridge CB2 8EA, United Kingdom
One Liberty Plaza, 20th Floor, New York, NY 10006, USA
477 Williamstown Road, Port Melbourne, VIC 3207, Australia
314–321, 3rd Floor, Plot 3, Splendor Forum, Jasola District Centre, New Delhi – 110025, India
103 Penang Road, #05–06/07, Visioncrest Commercial, Singapore 238467

Cambridge University Press is part of Cambridge University Press & Assessment, a department of the University of Cambridge.

We share the University's mission to contribute to society through the pursuit of education, learning and research at the highest international levels of excellence.

www.cambridge.org
Information on this title: www.cambridge.org/9781009581318
DOI: 10.1017/9781009581295

© Mark Feng Teng 2025

This publication is in copyright. Subject to statutory exception and to the provisions of relevant collective licensing agreements, no reproduction of any part may take place without the written permission of Cambridge University Press & Assessment.

When citing this work, please include a reference to the DOI 10.1017/9781009581295

First published 2025

A catalogue record for this publication is available from the British Library

ISBN 978-1-009-58131-8 Hardback
ISBN 978-1-009-58130-1 Paperback
ISSN 2632-4415 (online)
ISSN 2632-4407 (print)

Cambridge University Press & Assessment has no responsibility for the persistence or accuracy of URLs for external or third-party internet websites referred to in this publication and does not guarantee that any content on such websites is, or will remain, accurate or appropriate.

Metacognition in Language Teaching

Elements in Language Teaching

DOI: 10.1017/9781009581295
First published online: March 2025

Mark Feng Teng
Macao Polytechnic University
Author for correspondence: Mark Feng Teng, markteng@mpu.edu.mo

Abstract: Metacognition, the awareness and regulation of one's own learning process, is a cornerstone of effective language learning. This Element is a ground-breaking text that offers a comprehensive guide to incorporating metacognitive strategies into the teaching of reading, writing, vocabulary, and listening. This Element stands as a bridge between theoretical frameworks and actionable teaching practices, enabling educators to enhance their students' language proficiency in a holistic manner. This Element is replete with case studies, examples from diverse learning contexts, and evidence-based practices. It is an invaluable resource for language educators who aspire to cultivate independent learners capable of self-assessment and strategy adjustment. By fostering metacognitive awareness across all facets of language learning, this Element empowers students to take charge of their own learning journey, leading to more profound and lasting language mastery.

This Element also has a video abstract: www.cambridge.org/ELAT_Teng

Keywords: Metacognition in language teaching, Metacognitive awareness, Metacognition in reading, Metacognition in writing, Metacognition in vocabulary learning

© Mark Feng Teng 2025

ISBNs: 9781009581318 (HB), 9781009581301 (PB), 9781009581295 (OC)
ISSNs: 2632-4415 (online), 2632-4407 (print)

Contents

1 Introduction on Metacognition in Language Teaching   1

2 Understanding Metacognition   5

3 Metacognition in Reading   22

4 Metacognition in Writing   31

5 Metacognition in Listening   49

6 Metacognition in Vocabulary Learning   56

7 Assessing Metacognition   62

8 Conclusion on Metacognition in Language Teaching   70

    References   75

1 Introduction on Metacognition in Language Teaching

This Element was inspired by my experience at a forum on methodology in applied linguistics in Osaka, Japan. During the event, a teacher commented on the importance of my presentation on metacognition in language teaching and learning, urging me to delve deeper into this topic. This encouragement resonated with me, and I decided to explore the subject further through this Element for several reasons. First, I currently teach in Macao, where incorporating metacognition into language teaching and learning comes with substantial challenges; many students here struggle with motivation in language learning. I believe that fostering metacognitive awareness could provide useful strategies to help these students become more engaged, autonomous learners. However, I also believe that we need more understanding on this topic, especially in challenging situations where motivation is lacking. The cultural context of Macao, with its unique blend of Chinese and Portuguese influences, adds another layer of complexity to this issue. Unlike many other regions, students in Macao mostly do not face pressure from high-stakes testing and societal expectations. This is largely because the society and government have casinos as one of the biggest sources of income, which can further dampen their intrinsic motivation to learn languages. The relatively stable economic achievement provided by the casino industry might lead students to feel less urgency in pursuing academic excellence, including language proficiency. To address this, educators must explore innovative approaches that resonate with students' experiences and interests, potentially integrating technology and collaborative learning to spark curiosity and engagement. Additionally, professional development for teachers on how to effectively implement metacognitive strategies in the classroom could be crucial in overcoming these challenges. Ultimately, a deeper exploration of the interplay between metacognition and motivation in this context could lead to more effective teaching practices and improved language learning outcomes.

Second, I have an extensive track record of publications involving metacognition in language teaching. My research has delved deeply into how metacognitive strategies can enhance second language vocabulary acquisition and writing, providing insights into both theoretical frameworks and practical applications. These publications have explored various aspects of metacognition, such as self-regulation, self-efficacy, and strategic planning, and their impact on learners' ability to acquire and apply new language skills effectively. Now is an opportune time to share my findings with a broader audience, enabling readers to better understand this crucial matter.

Finally, although metacognition is a well-recognised topic in educational psychology, it has not received the attention it deserves in the context of language teaching. In educational psychology, metacognition is celebrated for its role in enhancing learning processes, promoting self-awareness, and improving problem-solving skills across various disciplines (Flavell, 1979). However, when it comes to language teaching, the application of metacognitive strategies remains underexplored and underutilised. After Wenden (1998) highlighted this issue in language learning, there still hasn't been sufficient attention given to it. This oversight is significant, given the potential benefits that metacognition can bring to language learners, such as improved comprehension, enhanced vocabulary acquisition, and greater overall language proficiency. The lack of emphasis on metacognition in language education may stem from traditional teacher-centred methods that prioritise rote memorisation and repetitive practice over reflective and strategic learning, particularly in the English as a Foreign Language (EFL) context. Such approaches often fail to engage learners in meaningful ways or to develop their ability to think critically about their own learning processes. Integrating metacognitive approaches into language curricula can empower students to take control of their learning, fostering a deeper understanding and more meaningful engagement with the language. Addressing this gap in attention could lead to innovative teaching practices that not only enhance language skills but also equip learners with lifelong learning strategies. By fostering a metacognitive mindset, educators can help students become more self-directed, adaptable, and effective learners, capable of navigating the complexities of language acquisition and beyond.

As mentioned earlier, interest in this area has grown following Wenden's (1998) seminal publication; however, comprehensive resources remain needed, which describe how to apply metacognitive strategies in language pedagogy (Rose, 2012). This Element aims to fill that gap by synthesising the extant literature, providing practical insights, and highlighting the role of metacognitive training in language learning. By doing so, I hope to contribute to the ongoing dialogue in language teaching and offer tools for educators seeking to improve students' language-learning experiences through enhanced metacognitive awareness.

At least three notable books have addressed metacognition in language teaching. The first is Goh and Vandergrift's (2021) work on metacognition in listening. They examine both the theory of metacognition in listening and the adoption of associated strategies in the English as a second language (ESL)/ English as a foreign language (EFL) classroom. The focus is on the often understudied area of second language communication skills, that is, listening. Goh and Vandergrift (2021) reviewed listening-related research, outlining how listening instruction has traditionally been delivered and pointing out the drawbacks of these approaches. Pitfalls include a lack of understanding of the

Metacognition in Language Teaching 3

listening process itself and an overemphasis on input comprehension as the exemplar of listening skills. The authors argued for a learner-centred approach to listening instruction that integrates metacognitive strategies. These techniques are meant to help learners understand how they learn, thus teaching students to self-correct and improve their overall listening experience.

The second one is Haukås et al.'s (2018) discussion of metacognition in language teaching and learning. This complete volume is divided into theoretical and empirical sections, offering a multifaceted view of metacognition. It covers a range of perspectives, including metalinguistic and multilingual awareness as well as language learning and teaching in both second-language (L2) and third-language (L3) settings. They also summarise empirical studies related to writing, teacher education, and classroom communication. Its breadth is remarkable: this work features numerous contexts and views on metacognition in language learning and teaching. One highlight of Haukås et al.'s (2018) work is their accentuation of the importance of metacognition in language teacher education. The authors advocate for a stronger focus on developing metacognitive skills among experienced and future teachers. They stress that fostering an interest in metacognition is essential for teachers to enhance their own instructional practices and to help students develop these critical skills. This process mandates knowledge sharing and collaboration.

The third one, authored by L. Teng (2022), offers an in-depth exploration of self-regulation within the realm of second language learning and teaching. This pivotal work applies self-regulation theory to language acquisition, presenting a groundbreaking conceptual framework designed to evaluate multidimensional self-regulated learning strategies. By connecting these strategies with social, psychological, and linguistic factors, Teng provides a holistic view of how learners can effectively manage their own language learning processes. She delves into the practical applications and contributions of self-regulated learning (SRL) to second and foreign language (L2) writing, examined from both sociocognitive and sociocultural perspectives. This work showcases a thorough and up-to-date review of the conceptual and methodological issues surrounding SRL, as well as the latest research on its application in L2 learning and teaching contexts. L. Teng's volume further details the design and outcomes of a comprehensive large-scale project that includes both observational and intervention studies, investigating SRL strategies in L2 writing. This research highlights the critical importance of a cross-disciplinary understanding of SRL strategies, emphasising their role in advancing theoretical frameworks and extending their applications to L2 education broadly, with a particular focus on L2 writing. Additionally, this work discusses various strategy questionnaires and their validation processes, offering valuable insights into the discussion of self-regulated learning strategies. By providing these tools and methodologies, L. Teng's work contributes significantly to enhancing the effectiveness of language education, empowering learners to become more autonomous and proficient in their language acquisition endeavours.

Contributing to the existing body of knowledge, this Element reports on metacognition in reading, writing, listening, and vocabulary learning along with the assessment of metacognition in language teaching. There is little doubt that metacognition is instrumental to effective language learning and teaching. Through this Element, readers will come to realise the importance of metacognitive awareness in language pedagogy. Successful language learners are aware of the complexities of the target language they hope to master, the hurdles involved in the learning process, their own beliefs about language learning and teaching, and techniques that can be employed to overcome these obstacles. The same principles apply to language educators: to deliver more impactful lessons, teachers must not only be aware of their pedagogical practices and beliefs but also understand how different instructional methods suit students' personal profiles and environments. It is similarly necessary to remember that teachers are lifelong learners themselves, continually refining their understanding of the language they teach and searching for ways to make their lessons more appealing and beneficial to students.

Against this backdrop, this Element represents a much-needed contribution to the field of language teaching, including listening, writing, reading, and vocabulary learning. Despite the limitations of insufficient information on understanding the role of metacognition in speaking, this Element spotlights the importance of metacognitive awareness across multiple domains of language education, emphasising its role in enhancing both teaching and learning processes. By highlighting the critical need for metacognitive skills, this Element provides ample justification for the topic's theoretical exploration and practical application. It underscores how metacognitive awareness can lead to more effective language acquisition by enabling learners to plan, monitor, and evaluate their learning strategies. Moreover, this Element addresses the essential need to cultivate metacognitive skills not only among learners but also among pre-service and in-service teachers. By doing so, it helps to bridge the gap between theory, research, practice, and assessment, ensuring that educational practices are informed by the latest insights and methodologies. This alignment is crucial for developing a more integrated approach to language teaching, where theoretical concepts are seamlessly translated into classroom strategies and assessment tools. This Element is indispensable for anyone involved in language teaching, as it contains tactical guidance for fostering metacognitive awareness. It offers educators practical strategies to enhance the general effectiveness of language teaching, equipping them with the tools to nurture independent, reflective, and strategic learners. By integrating these approaches into their teaching practices, educators can significantly improve learning outcomes and contribute to the development of lifelong language learning skills among their students.

2 Understanding Metacognition

Metacognition is key in distinguishing effective language learners from less effective ones; it significantly affects students' decision making and success in acquiring a language. Language teachers are crucial in nurturing students' metacognitive awareness, namely by modelling metacognitive strategies during instruction. It is equally critical for teachers to possess a metacognitive understanding of their pedagogical methods in order to enhance students' language-learning experiences. Thus, the comprehension of metacognition is imperative to consider.

2.1 An Understanding of Metacognition from Educational Psychology

2.1.1 Definition of Metacognition

The concept of metacognition has long intrigued educational psychologists, and its importance in academic achievement is well established. Metacognitive knowledge improves the quality and effectiveness of academic learning (Schraw, 1998). This awareness not only improves self-regulated learning (SRL; Wenden, 2002) but also fosters learner autonomy (Victori & Lockhart, 1995), allowing students to take charge of their educational journeys and adapt to various learning environments. Furthermore, metacognitive skills are closely linked to scholastic achievement, as they empower learners to set goals, monitor their progress, and adjust their approaches to overcome challenges (Zimmerman & Bandura, 1994). By cultivating these skills, students can achieve higher levels of academic success and develop the resilience needed to tackle complex tasks. Fairbanks et al. (2010) contended that teachers who recognise metacognition's place in learning can better support students' development. By integrating metacognitive strategies into their teaching practices, educators can create a more supportive learning environment that encourages students to reflect on their thinking, evaluate their understanding, and apply their knowledge more effectively.

Due to its interdisciplinary nature and multiple theoretical perspectives, metacognition has no universal definition. However, in the field of educational psychology, the description that Flavell provided in the 1970s is widely regarded as foundational. Known for his theory-of-mind approach, he explained metacognition as 'the active monitoring and consequent regulation and orchestration of these processes in relation to the cognitive objects or data on which learners bear, usually in the service of some concrete goal or objective' (Flavell, 1976, p. 232). A core feature of this definition is that metacognition involves applying the theory of mind to cognitive tasks.

The theory of mind refers to one's cognitive ability to 'attribute mental states, such as beliefs, desires, and intentions, to oneself and others' (Lockl & Schneider, 2006, p. 16). Boekaerts (1997) expanded on this notion by stating that metacognition encompasses not only a theory of mind but also a 'theory of self, theory of learning, and learning environments' (p. 165). Building on these ideas, Flavell (1979) further defined metacognition as learners' awareness of their cognitive and executive processes with the aim of regulating various aspects of cognitive activities. He proposed three domains within metacognition: metacognitive knowledge, metacognitive experiences, and metacognitive strategies. Additionally, Flavell (1979) conceptualised metacognition as consisting of four components: metacognitive knowledge, metacognitive experiences, goals, and strategy activation.

2.1.2 Frameworks on Understanding Metacognition

Flavell (1985) introduced a holistic, two-dimensional framework to clarify metacognition. These dimensions are knowledge of metacognition (person, task, and strategies) and regulation of metacognition (planning, monitoring, and evaluating). His model captures both the cognitive nature of metacognition and this concept's role in knowledge regulation. Many researchers have adopted the classification to operationalise metacognition. Flavell's framework affords teachers a richer sense of students' metacognition, enabling instructors to more readily facilitate change in students' learning processes and outcomes. For instance, learners' comprehension of person-oriented variables influences their decision making when choosing strategies, monitoring these techniques' application, and transferring them to new learning tasks. Similarly, learners' knowledge of task-related variables empowers them to select approaches suited to specific activities. Learners' understanding of different strategies also guides them in making informed decisions about options, ultimately enhancing the effectiveness of their educational endeavours. Understanding the notions of planning, monitoring, and evaluating is of utmost importance for teachers and learners alike. A solid grasp of planning allows teachers to develop well-structured lessons that align with desired learning outcomes. Moreover, by closely monitoring students' progress, teachers can identify individual strengths

Metacognition in Language Teaching 7

and weaknesses and offer targeted support to encourage optimal learning. Evaluation enables teachers to assess learning outcomes, provide timely and constructive feedback, and foster students' growth. Meanwhile, learners benefit from understanding planning, monitoring, and evaluating by being able to set clear and achievable goals, track their progress, and make necessary adjustments. They employ SRL strategies to appraise their own performance, reflect on their comprehension, and improve by taking ownership of their education and becoming self-directed learners.

Also in the realm of metacognition, scholars have embraced a framework that categorises metacognitive knowledge into three types based on respective processes: declarative, procedural, and conditional knowledge (Paris et al., 1984). Declarative knowledge refers to factual understanding about oneself (i.e., a sense of one's skills, intellectual capacities, affective factors, and cognitive abilities). For instance, learners may possess declarative knowledge when they recognise their strengths and weaknesses in a certain subject area or discover their preferred learning styles. Procedural knowledge, on the other hand, calls for making decisions about task implementation by employing proper strategies (Paris et al., 1984). Let us consider learning to swim. At first, despite receiving directions from an instructor, a learner may struggle to swim until they have practiced a few times. Repetition leads to this task becoming implicit knowledge, which resides in the learner's subconscious. Such knowledge is difficult to quantify; it arises from practice and experience. Conditional knowledge pertains to the decision-making process about when, where, and why specific strategies should be used to accomplish particular tasks (Schraw, 1998). This type of knowledge is crucial for applying suitable techniques and allocating resources efficiently. Conditional knowledge enables learners to act as guides in determining when and how strategies can be adopted to execute a task. For instance, a student may possess conditional knowledge when they recognise that using mnemonic devices is beneficial for memorising information and then identifies fitting contexts in which to deploy this approach.

According to Brown (1987), metacognitive regulation differs from metacognitive skills, as it refers to how people detect distracting internal and external stimuli in order to sustain effort over time for executive functions. Schraw (1998) elaborated on planning, monitoring, and evaluating. Planning involves one's ability to use appropriate strategies and resources to complete tasks. It reflects the thoughtful consideration of steps required to accomplish a goal and the successful coordination of one's approach. By engaging in careful planning, learners can optimise their efforts and increase their chances of success. Monitoring refers to one's capacity to check their performance during tasks; it involves keeping an eye on one's progress, identifying deviations or errors, and adjusting to stay on track. Effective monitoring allows learners to address issues as they arise, which helps learners stay engaged in the educational process. Evaluating calls for assessing one's regulatory processes and learning outcomes, namely by thinking about the utility of chosen strategies, the quality of one's work, and overall success in the learning experience. This metacognitive skill enables learners to analyse their own performance and make deliberate decisions for future improvements. Schraw and Dennison (1994) proposed two additional metacognitive strategies based on debugging and information management. Debugging strategies involve noting and rectifying lapses in comprehension and performance. Learners with this skill can acknowledge misconceptions, thus developing deeper understanding and more precise performance. Information management strategies pertain to processing, organising, elaborating, and summarising task-related information. These strategies aid learners in manipulating the information they encounter to promote comprehension and retention.

Anastasia Efklides has offered insight into metacognition as well. For example, Efklides (2001) stated that learners' metacognitive knowledge and metacognitive experiences are closely connected. These experiences correspond to learners' feelings about their own knowledge, their opinions about their own understanding, their perceptions of task difficulty, and their assessments of confidence and correctness when performing tasks. Numerous factors can influence learners' metacognitive experiences: task complexity; prior experiences; personal attributes (e.g., cognitive ability, personality, and self-concept); and, of course, metacognitive knowledge. Efklides (2006) further described metacognition as a higher-order cognitive model that interacts with object-level cognition through monitoring and control functions. The meta level receives input from the object level through monitoring, which then informs the control function to adapt cognitive processes accordingly. Metacognitive experiences are seen as complex inferential processes that reflect one's progress towards a goal; this feedback is delivered in either an affective or cognitive context. These experiences are critical in activating affective or cognitive regulatory loops, in turn guiding self-regulatory mechanisms. Efklides (2008) expanded on metacognition by specifying it across three domains in line with Flavell (1979): metacognitive knowledge, metacognitive experiences, and metacognitive strategies. In particular, metacognitive experiences encompass one's conscious awareness and feelings during information processing (e.g., the feeling of knowing, the effort involved, solutions' accuracy, perceived difficulties, familiarity with the content, and personal confidence). These experiences are crucial for individuals to assess task performance. Metacognitive knowledge and experiences contribute to the monitoring aspect of cognition, while metacognitive skills pertain to its control. In the learning process, one's metacognitive experiences – shaped by subjective and affective responses – can greatly affect one's general metacognitive framework. For example, feelings such as satisfaction or anxiety can influence a learner's future strategy use and shape their metacognitive knowledge. Metacognitive experiences play a significant role in the classroom, where students display a range of emotions. Efklides (2008) framed metacognition as a fully conscious endeavour, with people being entirely aware of their monitoring and control processes. She also argued that metacognition is individualised and that external factors minimally affect it; that is, metacognition represents a personal part of the learning process. The classification of metacognition's sub-components is important. If this concept concerns both how one monitors and controls their own thinking, then it naturally covers a suite of phenomena (e.g., introspective and self-regulatory processes). It is accordingly necessary to identify distinguishable sub-components of metacognition. Certain facets – namely knowledge, strategies, and experiences – constitute a classic framework.

2.1.3 Key Theoretical Stances

The subject of metacognition has drawn substantial attention from researchers and educators in various disciplines given its relevance to learning, problem solving, reasoning, and conceptual understanding across learners, topics, domains, tasks, and contexts. However, the challenge of comprehending metacognition becomes apparent as different definitions, constructs, assumptions, processes, and mechanisms are proposed. Azevedo (2020) contended that, despite clear progress in this field, more theoretical work is needed to cohesively define metacognition and its constituent parts. Veenman, van Hout-Wolters, and Afflerbach (2006) rightly stated that 'while there is consistent acknowledgement of the importance of metacognition, inconsistency marks the conceptualisation of the construct' (p. 4). Norman et al.'s (2019) review identified major advancements in metacognition research and summarised the term's definitions using three branches. The first branch revolves around the extent to which metacognition is a pre-conscious, pre-reflective, non-representational, or pre-verbal form of thinking. This line of enquiry explores the foundational aspects of metacognitive processes that occur before conscious awareness or introspection. The second branch shifts the focus from the mere existence of metacognitive thinking to understanding how people engage in metacognitive processes and proactively manage important tasks. This branch investigates the active regulation and control of cognitive processes through metacognition and explores how people monitor and alter their cognitive strategies to optimise learning and performance. The third branch concerns developmental aspects of metacognitive abilities across the lifespan, particularly whether these skills change with age. This research agenda considers how cognitive fluency and processing time may influence metacognitive functioning and whether metacognitive abilities decline in adulthood.

2.1.4 Reflection

Here, I have attempted to summarise metacognition based on themes and keywords from the literature. I hope this synthesis sheds light on the concept's intricacies. First, metacognition is often described as 'cognition about cognition', meaning that metacognition involves thinking about personal cognitive processes. It goes beyond simply engaging in cognitive activities to being aware of and monitoring one's thinking. Metacognition has also been deemed 'information-based', which suggests that various factors – including conscious and non-conscious ones – affect metacognitive processes. For example, the speed at which an answer comes to mind or a person's familiarity with a task domain can shape metacognitive judgements. A dynamic interplay thus exists between conscious and non-conscious aspects of metacognition. Furthermore, metacognitive feelings are typically described as 'experience-based': these feelings refer to one's subjective perceptions of their own cognitive processes and encompass elements such as the feeling of knowing, the effort involved in a task, solution accuracy, obstacles, content familiarity, and confidence. These experiences grant people valuable feedback on their cognitive performance. Metacognitive processes are conscious in both cases, as metacognition involves higher-order mental representations indicative of consciousness. People therefore need to be cognisant of their own thinking and to perform reflective processes that transcend automatic or non-conscious cognitive activities.

2.2 An Understanding of Metacognition in Language Teaching and Learning

2.2.1 Definition of Metacognition in Language Teaching and Learning

The field of language teaching has increasingly acknowledged the role of metacognitive awareness for learners. Metacognitive awareness is crucial in language teaching and learning, especially in foreign-language and L2 education. Educators who prioritise cognitive strategies and self-directed language learning know the significance of incorporating metacognitive awareness into curricula. Researchers have investigated the link between metacognition and successful language learners (Anderson, 2008). Common tenets of metacognitive instructional models include activating students' prior knowledge, reflecting on their knowledge and learning

Metacognition in Language Teaching 11

goals, explaining and modelling strategies (i.e., by the teacher), and involving students in setting goals for monitoring the learning process. The teacher plays a critical part in explaining, modelling, and creating an environment conducive to reflective discussions. However, metacognition has not yet received the attention it deserves within language teaching and learning.

Wenden (1987) may be the first to highlight the roles of metacognition in language learning and teaching; he played a pioneering role in this field. Building on Flavell's work, Wenden identified three types of metacognitive knowledge: person knowledge, task knowledge, and strategy knowledge. His contributions to the realm of metacognition in language learning and teaching underlined these categories' importance. Person knowledge refers to one's understanding of their cognitive processes, strengths, and weaknesses in relation to language learning. It involves self-awareness and self-reflection, allowing individuals to recognise their preferred learning styles, language aptitude, and motivation levels. By developing person knowledge, learners become more attuned to their own educational needs and can make informed decisions about their language learning approaches. Task knowledge pertains to the purpose, demands, and requirements of specific language learning tasks. It involves being able to evaluate task objectives and to identify the resources required for completion. Task knowledge enables learners to approach language learning tasks with a clear sense of what is expected and how to achieve desired outcomes. Strategy knowledge encompasses the awareness and use of learning techniques for effective language acquisition (e.g., to enhance language learning efficiency); this type of knowledge equips learners with a repertoire of strategies, such as note taking, summarising, self-assessment, and goal setting, so they may choose which tactics to employ in different language learning contexts. Learners who nurture these forms of metacognitive knowledge can take more active, autonomous roles in their language learning.

2.2.2 Frameworks on Understanding Metacognition in Language Teaching and Learning

In Wenden's (1998) framework, metacognitive knowledge should be viewed as a prerequisite for SRL. Such knowledge guides planning (i.e., early in one's learning process) and monitoring processes as one moves through learning tasks. It comprises self-observation, assessment of progress and challenges, and decisions about remediation. Furthermore, metacognitive knowledge serves as a criterion for appraising a finished learning task. However, metacognitive knowledge alone may be insufficient for certain aspects of planning: domain knowledge plays a complementary and essential role. Metacognitive knowledge serves two distinct functions. First, it is motivational in that it energises the self-regulation involved in learning. Second, it is cognitively oriented because it directly moulds those processes. Language educators should acknowledge the significance of incorporating knowledge about learning into tasks designed to help language learners build learning strategies. People with strong metacognitive awareness are better prepared to face the obstacles inherent to second language learning. They also tend to demonstrate a firm belief in their ability to succeed in language learning and take proactive measures to realise their educational pursuits (Wenden, 1998). Recognising the role of metacognition in second language learning can hold value for second language acquisition. Numerous attributes, such as age, language aptitude, and motivation, can influence one's extent of person-based knowledge. Bringing metacognitive awareness into language teaching and learning enables students to grapple with challenges, trust in their language learning skills, and work towards attaining associated goals.

The process of gaining declarative knowledge is closely related to metalinguistic awareness. Metalinguistic awareness refers to one's ability 'to consider language not just as a means of expressing ideas or communicating with others but also as an object of inquiry' (Gass & Selinker, 2008, p. 359). It involves introspection about the structure, rules, and components of language itself. Learners possessing metalinguistic awareness can develop language awareness, which then enhances their metalinguistic awareness. Language awareness encompasses explicit knowledge of language and involves conscious perception and sensitivity to the learning, teaching, and use of language (Svalberg, 2007). It goes beyond deploying language as a communication tool; people with language awareness have a conscious understanding of, and desire to explore, language's structures, functions, and conventions. Within the area of metacognition, explicit knowledge about language learning processes falls under declarative metacognitive knowledge. This knowledge involves being aware of the strategies and principles that facilitate language learning (e.g., knowledge of learning techniques, learning styles, and language acquisition approaches). Declarative metacognitive knowledge enables individuals to deliberately reflect on their learning processes, make educated decisions about their learning tactics, and adapt these approaches to suit their needs. Learners obtain explicit knowledge about language structures and functions through metalinguistic awareness and language awareness. This understanding supports their metacognition concerning language learning processes, and they can navigate their language learning journey more effectively. Learners with explicit knowledge can also actively track their progress, measure their language proficiency, and choose language learning strategies wisely.

2.2.3 Key Theoretical Stances

There are some key theoretical stances regarding metacognition in language teaching and learning. Anderson (2002, 2008) outlined five components of metacognition about learning to be developed in the language classroom: (1) preparing and planning for learning (i.e., students reflect on their goals and identify strategies to achieve them); (2) allowing students to make conscious decisions about their learning strategies and processes; (3) monitoring strategy use and encouraging students to track the effectiveness of their chosen techniques; (4) orchestrating diverse approaches (i.e., teaching students to combine multiple strategies); and (5) evaluating strategy use and learning (i.e., cyclically asking questions about goals, techniques used, and possible alternatives). Anderson emphasised that these components work together to enhance language learners' metacognitive skills.

Rose (2012) criticised the current measurement of language learning strategies, arguing that available practices are usually unreliable. He called for clearer definitions of strategic learning and the development of more accurate and qualitative instruments to assess this construct. Rose further contended that it is essential to examine strategic learning not only based on a student's self-regulation during a learning task but also in terms of their cognitive and behavioural strategies. Research frameworks that include both self-regulation and strategy use need to be explored to fully illustrate strategic learning. Additionally, theories must remain flexible to encourage new models of strategic learning. The need for strategic learning highlights the importance of metacognitive awareness in language teaching.

Haukås (2018) defined metacognition as 'an awareness of and reflections about one's knowledge, experiences, emotions and learning in the contexts of language learning and teaching' (p. 13). Haukås also linked metacognitive awareness with language awareness. Metacognition refers to broad reflections on one's knowledge, experiences, emotions, and learning across all domains, whereas language awareness pertains to reflections in a trio of sub-domains: language, language learning, and language teaching. These domains are interconnected, and metacognition in language teaching often involves simultaneous reflection in all three. Investigations into teachers' and learners' beliefs, the use of learning strategies, metalinguistic and multilingual awareness, intercultural awareness, and self-efficacy all represent aspects of metacognition. Such analyses shed light on how people perform metacognitive processes in language learning and teaching contexts. By examining their own beliefs, students and teachers can gain insights into their personal cognitive processes, attitudes, and motivations around language learning. Learning strategy use involves metacognitive decision making, where people consciously choose and deploy techniques to enhance their language learning outcomes (Oxford, 1990). Metalinguistic and multilingual awareness concern one's ability to scrutinise the structure, applications, and relationships between languages. Intercultural awareness entails reflecting on the cultural dimensions of language and communication. Finally, self-efficacy relates to one's belief in their ability to succeed in language learning tasks (F. Teng, 2024d).

L. Teng and Zhang (2022) asserted that self-regulation principles and metacognitive awareness practices can enrich L2/foreign language learning and teaching. L. Teng (2022) bridged SRL with language learning strategies, stressing the learning process and students' pivotal roles within it. 'SRL' and 'language learning strategies' are multifaceted terms that include cognitive, metacognitive, social-behavioural, and motivational components. This rich framework allows for the incorporation of control mechanisms related to cognition, behaviour, the environment, and motivation. Scholars can therefore inspect various dimensions of learners' SRL development. For instance, L. Teng (2024) pointed out the importance of exploring motivational regulation and social behaviour in L2 writing settings. The process of L2 writing can be evaluated through a multidimensional lens, including determining how learners set goals and subsequently regulate their cognition, motivation, and behaviour during the writing process. This point of view acknowledges that these components are often influenced by learners' goals and diverse contextual features. Scholars and educators can gain valuable insights into the metacognitive aspects of language learning by considering these interconnected factors. L. Teng's ideas reinforce the significance of metacognition in language learning and teaching. By contemplating the interplay between SRL and language learning strategies, educators can promote learners' autonomy, self-regulation, and strategic thinking. This understanding fosters instructional interventions that support learners in becoming proficient language users. Metacognitive practices also convey the need to empower learners to be active participants in their own learning (i.e., by setting goals, tracking their progress, and adjusting when necessary). As Zhang and Zhang (2018) said, metacognition – described as one's awareness of oneself, the task at hand, employed strategies, and personal readiness – is fundamental to students' agency and independence.

F. Teng et al. (2022) assembled a model to demystify metacognition, delineating this construct as the monitoring and control of cognition (see Figure 1). This framework maintains that metacognition operates on two principal levels: the observational level, where one tracks and assesses their cognitive activities; and the managerial level, where one fine-tunes these activities. This dual functionality underscores metacognition's role in fostering one's conscious awareness and mastery over cognitive functions. F. Teng et al. (2022) further

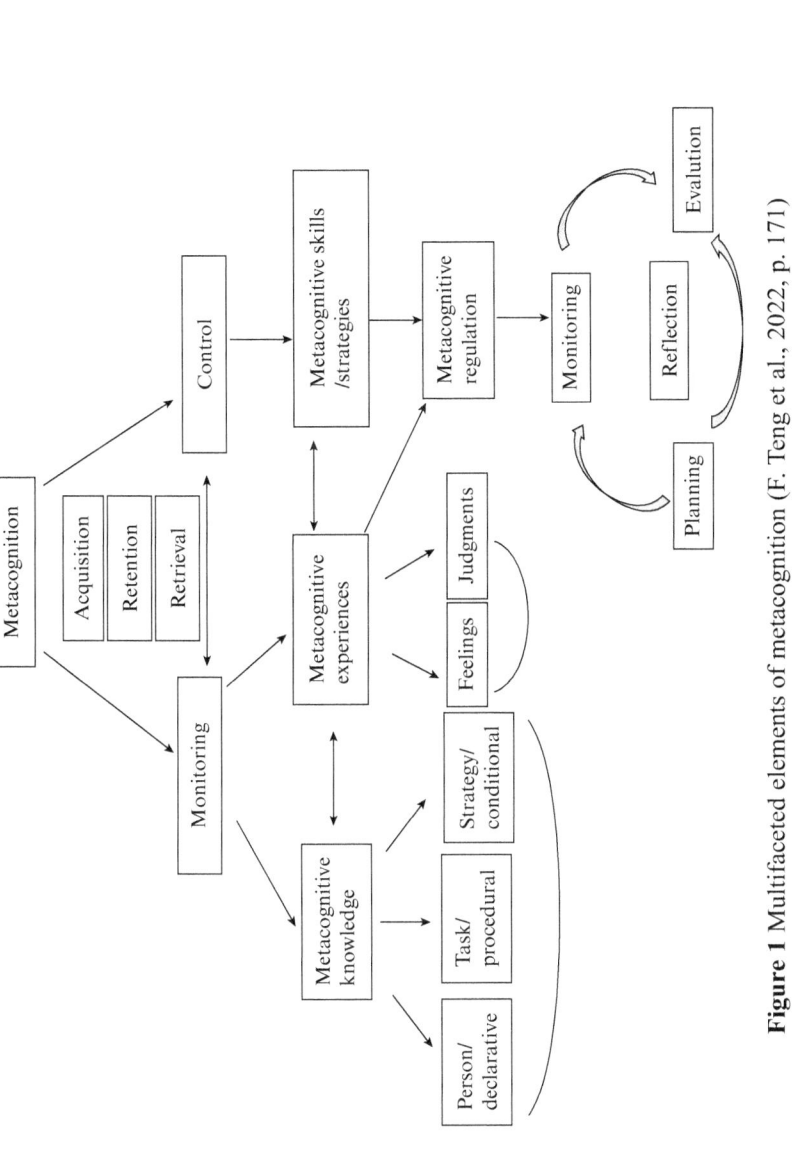

Figure 1 Multifaceted elements of metacognition (F. Teng et al., 2022, p. 171)

separated metacognition into three stages – acquisition, retention, and retrieval – that connect the observational and managerial dimensions. The model posits that metacognition is complex and has three interwoven domains: metacognitive knowledge (awareness of one's cognitive processes); metacognitive experiences (one's lived subjective experience of cognition); and metacognitive skills (one's application of strategies such as planning, monitoring, and evaluation). Central to this triad is the act of reflection, which is crucial for the cyclical process of planning, monitoring, and evaluating. F. Teng (2023a) expanded the discourse on metacognition by emphasising its deeply personal nature. F. Teng (2023a) noted that metacognition is not merely a set of abstract cognitive processes but a reflection of a person's evolving understanding and command over their own thinking and learning. This attribute is pivotal in educational settings, therapeutic contexts, and self-improvement; it dictates how one approaches new information and challenges. F. Teng (2023a) also elaborated on the symbiotic relationship between the pillars of metacognition (i.e., metacognitive knowledge, experiences, and skills). Metacognitive knowledge – one's understanding of their cognitive strengths, weaknesses, and strategies – is the basis upon which metacognitive experiences are built. These real-time, conscious experiences of cognition inform ongoing learning. Metacognitive skills, including the capacities to plan, monitor, and appraise one's cognitive strategies, are honed through applying knowledge and reflecting on one's experiences. Moreover, F. Teng (2023a) argued that this tripartite framework is not static but rather develops with practice. Individuals become more adept at deploying metacognitive strategies as they perform complex tasks, leading to a more sophisticated understanding of their learning processes. This iterative reflection and adaptation make metacognition a powerful ally in language learning.

Another interesting aspect of metacognition is that it possesses trait-like and state-like elements (Sato, 2022). This dichotomy is key for understanding how metacognitive abilities can vary between and within people over time. Metacognition, as a trait, refers to enduring qualities that define an individual's usual approach to learning. Some learners naturally engage in metacognitive thinking more regularly than others. Numerous factors can contribute to this tendency, including prior educational experiences, personal dispositions towards reflection, and innate cognitive abilities. Trait-like metacognition is relatively stable across settings and tasks, shaping how a person typically interacts with new information and problem-solving situations. A trait-like metacognitive approach during language learning might manifest in the habitual use of specific techniques for planning, monitoring, and evaluating one's own language development. Certain learners might consistently self-assess

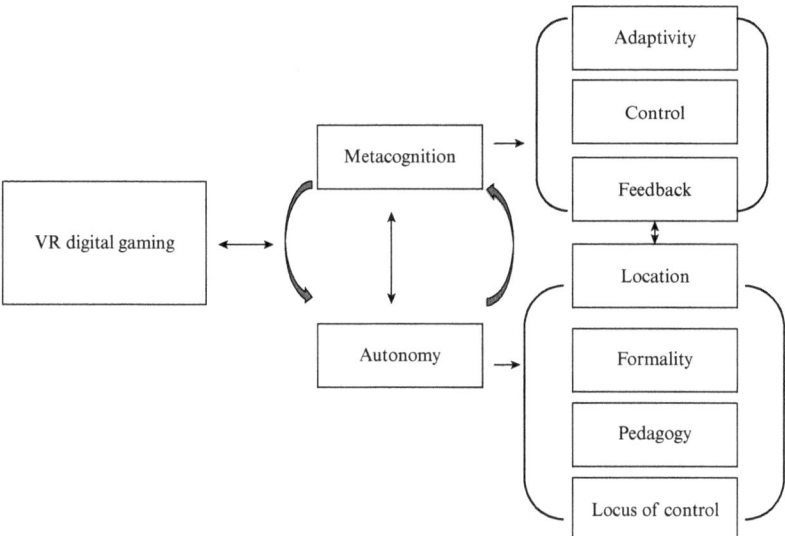

Figure 2 Metacognition and autonomy in virtual reality digital gaming (F. Teng, 2024a)

their progress in vocabulary acquisition or regularly reflect on their reading comprehension strategies. Conversely, the state of metacognition is more variable and context-dependent. A learner might exhibit strong metacognitive skills under particular circumstances (e.g., during a structured writing task where they are actively planning and revising their work) but not others (e.g., an impromptu speaking exercise). State-like metacognition is dynamic and can be enhanced or suppressed by issues such as stress, motivation, or perceived task difficulty. Language teachers can foster state-like metacognitive engagement among students by designing activities that prompt metacognitive thinking and by creating a classroom environment that encourages introspection and self-regulation.

F. Teng (2024a) proposed a framework (Figure 2) that elucidates the operational dynamics of students participating in virtual reality digital gaming. Central to this framework is an emphasis on metacognitive awareness for fostering learners' autonomy and vice versa. The reciprocal relationship between metacognition and autonomy highlights individuals' capacity to self-regulate and navigate learning experiences within virtual reality digital gaming contexts.

2.2.4 Reflection

In my attempt to summarise and understand the intricate dynamics of metacognition, I have come to realise that it is not merely an abstract concept but a practical tool that can transform the educational landscape. The increasing acknowledgement of metacognitive awareness in the field of language teaching highlights its necessity for learners to effectively harness their resources, identify linguistic challenges, and set achievable goals. This understanding resonates with my experiences in language education, where fostering metacognitive skills has proven essential in guiding students towards autonomy and success. The ability for students to reflect on their cognitive processes is crucial in enabling them to take charge of their learning journeys.

As an educator, I have witnessed first hand the transformative power of incorporating metacognitive strategies into curricula. It has become evident that when students are encouraged to activate prior knowledge, reflect on their learning goals, and engage in goal-setting, they develop a deeper understanding of their learning processes. This approach not only enhances their academic achievements but also prepares them for lifelong learning. The theoretical frameworks and insights have further enriched my understanding of how metacognitive awareness can be cultivated in language classrooms. The frameworks underscore the importance of creating a language learning environment where reflective discussions are encouraged, and where students are guided in developing their metacognitive skills. However, despite its recognised importance, metacognition still lacks the attention it deserves within language teaching and learning. This reflection has reinforced my commitment to advocating for its integration into language teaching and learning practices.

2.3 An Understanding of Metacognition Based on My Teaching and Research Experiences

I currently teach at Macao Polytechnic University. Macao is a unique region whose residents enjoy numerous privileges, including priority access to educational institutions and job opportunities with high salaries. The term 'job hunting' may not be entirely appropriate here, as many positions are reserved for Macao residents. Consequently, students in Macao seldom face great stress in terms related to their schooling or employment. The most perplexing aspect of language teaching in Macao is student involvement – many learners lack interest, drive, and incentive, and no strong communities of practice exist to promote engagement. Both the imagined and practiced communities for these students come with a lack of pressure; activities such as watching Netflix, browsing YouTube, and sleeping are prevalent. This alignment between the imagined and practiced communities affords students a consistent identity and position. However, mainland students encounter a disparity: their imagined community is one of university life, whereas their practiced community resembles a primary-school environment. This discrepancy can easily lead to an identity crisis. I therefore propose a novel conceptualisation of metacognition in language teaching and learning. Metacognition in language learning is partly based on seeking awareness as an agent of one's language learning, during which identity, position, and self-reflection are being promoted to enhance learning outcomes.

When I struggle to derive inspiration from teaching, I seek solace in research. However, the community in Macao does not seem to be research-oriented either. My imagined community would ideally offer ample feedback and support for conducting research. The reality is, for me, sadly different. Many of my colleagues show little interest in research and prefer instead to remain comfortable, as evidenced by comments like 'I only like my comfort zone', 'Please help us publish everything so we can rest more', 'Don't send me any academic posts – too much pressure', and 'Can I lay down like this for the rest of my life?' Given this atmosphere, I have been compelled to seek alternative communities of practice. For instance, connecting with friends and work partners at the Kansai Methodology Research Forum grants me the intellectual stimulation I seek; there, I can converse with others who are genuinely committed to research and academic progress. Thus, in my eyes, metacognition in research involves an awareness that positions the researcher as a seeker of knowledge. This sense extends beyond one's immediate surroundings. Interfacing with a broader academic community can enhance scholarship and personal growth.

2.4 Critical Issues

Several critical issues still stand to be explored upon perusing the literature on metacognition.

2.4.1 Metacognition and Age

The study of metacognition and its relationship to age has evolved over time. Early work in the 1970s mostly covered children's metamemory and their understanding of person, task, and strategy variables. Scholars investigating theory of mind subsequently delved into children's initial metacognitive knowledge, specifically the awareness of mental states such as desires and intentions. This exploration widened the scope of research to task-related cognitive processes meant to improve performance and track progress. Metacognition has been described as 'knowledge about knowledge', 'thoughts about thoughts", or "reflections about actions', all of which typify its self-reflective nature (Weinert, 1987, p. 8). Flavell (1979) pointed out the interconnectedness between the three facets of metacognition, where metacognitive knowledge informs the selection and use of metacognitive skills for specific people and cognitive tasks.

Researchers have aimed to understand the critical period for the establishment of metacognitive awareness. Insights suggest that metacognitive thinking may begin as soon as infancy and continue to develop throughout early childhood (Brinck & Liljenfors, 2013). Yet the matter of whether metacognitive abilities decline with age is up for debate. Interestingly, older adults have been found to outperform younger adults on some metacognitive tasks and can adapt and acquire metacognitive skills as needed (Pennequin et al., 2010). These patterns raise a question: are age-induced changes in metacognition primarily developmental or learning-related? Supplemental studies could clarify this issue (Hertzog, 2016).

2.4.2 Metacognition and Cognition

Metacognition, which is often mistaken for cognition, is distinct among cognitive processes. It is the scientific study of one's thinking about their own cognition, while cognition itself delves into aspects such as memory, attention, language comprehension, reasoning, learning, problem solving, and decision making. Metacognition's multidimensionality enables people to acquire domain-related knowledge and regulatory skills, empowering them to control cognitive processes across multiple domains (Schraw, 2001). In addition to its scientific definition, metacognition can be interpreted as one's awareness of and reflection on their knowledge, experiences, emotions, and learning in all areas. This broad understanding emphasises the introspective character of metacognition and its potential impacts on self-regulation and self-directed learning. Flavell (1979) distinguished between metacognitive and cognitive activities: the former category involves learners' planning, reflecting, monitoring, and evaluation of their learning processes; the latter focuses on acquiring information, clarifying concepts, and engaging in complex mental tasks (e.g., planning and executing activities). This differentiation underlines the active, self-reflective nature of metacognition and its roles in refining learning strategies and metacognitive regulation.

One compelling argument for the importance of metacognition lies in teachability. Educators can employ numerous strategies to cultivate students' metacognitive abilities. For instance, by using the 'think-aloud' method, instructors can guide students through problem solving while verbally expressing their thoughts and decision-making strategies. This technique allows learners to observe metacognitive processes in action and develop an understanding of productive problem solving. Modelling coping skills and resilience in the face

Metacognition in Language Teaching 21

of adversity is another powerful way to enhance metacognition. By demonstrating personal mistakes, perseverance, and adaptive strategies, educators provide students with insights into metacognitive regulation and the significance of metacognitive strategies. Engaging students in discussions about problem solving fosters metacognitive reflection. In being prompted to articulate their thought processes, students can better acknowledge their cognitive methods and refine those tactics accordingly. Concept mapping, reminder checklists, self-questioning, annotated drawings, and reciprocal teaching are additional ways to nurture metacognition. These techniques encourage students to actively deploy metacognitive processes, such as organising information, self-monitoring, and reflecting on personal learning strategies. However, cognition is not always easily taught.

2.4.3 Inconsistencies in Understanding Metacognition across Disciplines

Metacognition covers a range of areas that people control and monitor. Reasons for studying it vary by discipline. The field of early childhood studies stresses metacognitive activities related to managing human interaction and predicting the environmental conditions children are learning to navigate. This perspective recognises the importance of metacognition in social interaction and environmental adaptation during early development. Experimental cognitive psychology, in taking another tack, seeks to describe the information-processing antecedents underlying metacognitive feelings: researchers in this discipline strive to uncover the cognitive processes and mechanisms that give rise to metacognitive experiences and judgements (Koriat, 2007). Cognitive neuropsychology assumes a different approach by investigating the brain regions involved in metacognitive processing. Through neuroscientific methods, scholars aim to identify the neural correlates and mechanisms behind metacognition (Fleming et al., 2012). Personality psychology explores individual differences and their implications for metacognitive expression. Educational psychology emphasises metacognitive activities that facilitate effective learning and functioning in academic settings; this viewpoint strives to specify interventions that enhance learning outcomes and metacognitive regulation (Dimmitt & McCormick, 2012).

Metacognition also plays a crucial role in language teaching (Sato, 2022; F. Teng, 2023a; Zhang & Zhang, 2018). Language learners engage in metacognitive activities to monitor and regulate their language acquisition. These students are trained to be aware of their own language proficiency, set learning goals, plan study strategies, track their comprehension and production of language, and evaluate their progress. Metacognitive strategies in language learning involve reflecting on one's language abilities, identifying areas of strength and weakness, and implementing appropriate techniques to improve one's language skills. Relevant tactics may include self-questioning, self-monitoring, self-evaluation, and self-regulation.

2.5 Summary

This section has discussed multiple perspectives on metacognition by transitioning from the wider field of educational psychology to the more narrow domain of language learning and teaching. I hope that this background on metacognition will inspire researchers, language teacher educators, teacher trainees, and practicing language instructors. I encourage all professionals in these roles to start or continue investigating metacognition in language learning and teaching. There is a pressing need to centre metacognition within language teacher education programmes. Experienced and prospective teachers alike should be genuinely committed to developing their own metacognitive skills and fostering metacognition in their students. However, these goals require shared knowledge among all stakeholders in language education. Only through collaboration can a robust foundation be established for metacognitive practices. By recognising the vital part that metacognition plays in language learning and teaching, educators can empower students to become more self-regulated and autonomous in their language learning journeys. Metacognition equips people with the tools to reflect on their cognitive processes, set goals, choose appropriate strategies, monitor their progress, and adjust as needed. These skills are invaluable for lifelong language learning and can greatly increase the effectiveness and efficiency of language instruction.

3 Metacognition in Reading

Significant attention has been directed towards reading, particularly in understanding how L2 readers utilise their metacognitive knowledge to extract meaning from texts. Recognising that students' strategies represent conscious efforts to enhance their language skills and comprehension (Oxford, 1996; Rose, 2012), it becomes evident that metacognition plays an essential role in reading. By acknowledging this, educators can identify and impart successful strategies to less proficient readers, thereby improving their reading skills. Metacognitive knowledge, such as how students apply strategies in their EFL reading development, is crucial for effective reading instruction. Importantly, societal variations in target-language exposure and literacy traditions can influence reading excellence. This section argues that contextualising learners' metacognitive knowledge is vital for preparing them to apply this knowledge effectively, thereby enhancing their reading efficiency in real-life contexts.

3.1 Understanding the Role of Metacognition in Reading

Understanding the theoretical rationale of metacognition is fundamental to appreciating its role in reading. Metacognition involves awareness and regulation of one's cognitive processes, which is crucial for effective reading comprehension. It enables readers to plan, monitor, and evaluate their understanding as they engage with a text. This self-awareness allows readers to adapt their strategies to better comprehend and retain information, making reading a more purposeful and dynamic process.

Pedagogical support is known to be useful for devising strategies for meaningful reading. Learners' metacognitive knowledge about strategy use while learning to read appears critical for their reading efficiency and confidence building (Lehtonen, 2000). According to McLeod and McLaughlin (1986), reading is not a passive activity during which one simply extracts meaning from written text; it is instead 'an active and interactive process where the reader uses their language knowledge to predict and construct meaning based on the text' (p. 114). Readers who clearly perceive a reading task's metacognitive aspects are more likely to employ diverse strategies to process the text compared with those who lack such awareness. This perspective provides a basis for grasping metacognition in reading.

If metacognition is conceived as the practice of reflecting on and regulating one's learning, then in the reading context, it involves the student engaging in critical thinking about their own comprehension as they progress through a text. The reader becomes conscious of their cognitive experience and monitors their understanding. A core element of reading comprehension is achieving deep understanding, which goes beyond literal comprehension and factual knowledge to involve placing information in context. Individuals must connect this information to prior knowledge and then interpret, analyse, and compare it to their pre-existing understanding to potentially amend their understanding. This point also reflects the criticality of metacognition for reading. Related instruction focuses on mastering cognitive skills and developing automaticity in decoding, ultimately leading to reading fluency.

Previous work (Wen & Johnson, 1997) has shown that successful and unsuccessful EFL students' learning strategies are distinct. Strategy use resides on a continuum, with variations being tied to learners' language proficiency and skills. Strategy use ranges from ineffective to effective, and the perceived adoption of techniques may shift by task. Zhang (2001) tracked EFL learners' metacognitive awareness in reading via a semi-structured interview guide meant to elicit participants' metacognitive knowledge of strategy use. The approach followed Flavell's (1987) framework of metacognition. Participants' metacognitive knowledge of EFL reading was classified into three groups: person, task, and strategy. The data were coded based on audio recordings from the semi-structured interviews. Findings revealed that EFL learners' use of metacognitive reading strategies varied with proficiency levels: individuals with higher reading scores were more aware of reading strategies, whereas those with lower reading scores applied different reading strategies less proficiently. Among the evaluated techniques, comprehension monitoring was one of the most beneficial for readers. Zhang's study provided evidence for the role of metacognition in reading comprehension. Metacognition encompasses both knowledge and regulatory skills that help control one's cognitive processes. The results also suggest that aspects of metacognition, knowledge, and regulation are instrumental to reading; participants' understanding of grammatical and discoursal relationships was a prerequisite for accurate text comprehension. EFL readers must possess metacognitive strategic knowledge. Recognising the importance of such knowledge can drive students to reflect on their EFL learning experiences and thus increase their metacognitive skills.

Research has consistently highlighted a robust relationship between metacognitive instruction and reading proficiency. Scholars have found that people with stronger reading skills tend to display stronger metacognitive skills. Targeted metacognitive instruction can also improve one's reading ability. Zhang et al. (2008) focused on eighteen primary school students and shed further light on this correlation. The authors observed that learners could be guided to develop metacognitive strategies for reading comprehension. The young readers demonstrated a commendable ability to employ flexible, appropriate reading techniques. However, students' choices were contingent on language proficiency: higher-proficiency learners at higher grade levels exhibited a wider repertoire of reading strategies. These proficient readers could activate prior knowledge, make connections with the text, identify text structures, pose questions about the content, determine contextual information, and summarise their readings. Notably, the students also reported their thoughts while reading. These findings present practical ways for teachers to help students understand main parts of the reading process. By making students aware of the requirements of learning to read, educators can empower them to self-regulate their own reading experiences. Students hence need to develop comprehension strategies that bolster their text-based understanding and prepare them to navigate reading tasks more fluidly.

The significance of metacognitive instruction in reading extends to Chinese young learners as well. Teng (2020a) examined how metacognitive reading strategy instruction among Hong Kong English language learners improved their reading comprehension. The study involved twenty-five fifth graders. Data were collected from the notes learners took while reading, learners' post-reading reflection reports, teacher-facilitated group discussions, and two types of reading tests. The young students were taught a combination of strategies intended to gradually foster independent reading skills. The intervention unfolded in three stages: read and answer, reflect, and report and discuss. Participants identified twenty metacognitive knowledge factors that positively influenced their reading experiences. Furthermore, compared with students in the control group who did not receive metacognitive instruction, the intervention group attained higher scores on reading comprehension. These results provide support for the hypothesis that metacognitive knowledge enables learners to recognise when, why, and how to adapt their strategic choices. Students can then plan, monitor, and evaluate their reading processes more effectively.

Other studies, such as that by F. Teng and Zhang (2021), have longitudinally investigated the role of metacognitive knowledge in reading and writing. These efforts have revealed that learners' metacognitive knowledge (as well as their reading and writing proficiency) evolves throughout primary school. This developmental process is cumulative and features widening personal differences over time. Additionally, positive associations have been observed between one's initial levels of metacognitive knowledge, reading proficiency, and writing performance and the subsequent growth rates of each. These results convey dynamic relationships between metacognitive knowledge, reading proficiency, and writing proficiency throughout primary school. Specifically, a direct correlation has emerged between metacognitive knowledge and reading comprehension: improvements in metacognitive knowledge correspond to improvements in reading comprehension and vice versa. Baker's (2017) assertion that successful reading comprehension involves building a coherent mental model of a text supports this relationship. Learners who struggle to construct such a mental model may encounter difficulties when evaluating their meaning-making process while reading – hence the reciprocal association between metacognitive knowledge and reading comprehension. F. Teng and Zhang's (2021) study is unique in that it produced tentative support for the cyclical development of metacognitive knowledge and reading comprehension. This pattern implies that as young learners' metacognitive knowledge increases over time, their reading comprehension should increase as well. That tendency underscores the need to nurture students' metacognitive awareness and knowledge; doing so can promote reading comprehension in the long term.

A review of literature on metacognition in reading reveals that reading comprehension is a complex process requiring students to develop an awareness of print. This understanding can be achieved by cultivating metacognitive knowledge, which enables students to monitor their understanding and engage in reflective thinking about the text. Available research suggests a causal relationship between metacognitive instruction and reading proficiency; that is, people with stronger reading skills usually possess stronger metacognitive skills. Targeted metacognitive instruction may also improve reading ability. Despite empirical evidence of this relationship, correlation does not equate to causation: research using rigorous experimental designs remains necessary to definitively link metacognitive instruction with reading proficiency. Furthermore, although scholars have described EFL learners' varied use of metacognitive reading strategies based on language proficiency, more stands to be uncovered about these learners' specific techniques. Insights into effective methods for teaching and cultivating metacognitive strategies would be invaluable in enhancing reading instruction for EFL learners.

A summary of information in the above-mentioned studies can be summarised in the following Table 1.

3.2 Critical Issues

3.2.1 How Can Metacognitive Instruction Facilitate Reading?

Metacognition plays a key part in reading and prompts particular questions: How do students' monitoring and regulation processes influence their reading outcomes? More importantly, how can instruction support these reading processes? A major aspect of this field entails understanding who performs monitoring and regulation, when these processes occur, the environmental factors that stimulate them, and how they correlate to reading performance. Given the educational potential of metacognition, many studies have explored interventions designed to enhance reading skills – especially these treatments' impacts on students' reading abilities (e.g., Urban et al., 2023).

Metacognitive instruction, which can be broadly defined as pedagogical approaches aimed at improving domain-general, higher-order thinking processes in reading, seeks to develop in students self-regulatory strategies that foster engaged, strategic, and metacognitive comprehension. Yet teachers often face challenges to the scaffolded incorporation of reading strategies into daily classroom instruction. Planning is a critical stage preceding reading: strategic readers establish goals (e.g., remembering or comprehension), scan the text to gather information about it, activate prior knowledge, choose suitable strategies, allocate sufficient resources (e.g., reading time), and predict outcomes (Pressley & Gaskins, 2006).

Table 1 Key understanding of metacognition in reading

Aspect	Key understanding	References
Pedagogical support	Pedagogical support is essential for developing strategies that facilitate meaningful reading. It helps learners build metacognitive knowledge, which is crucial for reading efficiency and confidence.	Lehtonen (2000)
Nature of reading	Reading is an active and interactive process where readers use their language knowledge to predict and construct meaning. Metacognitive awareness allows readers to employ diverse strategies for processing texts.	McLeod and McLaughlin (1986)
Longitudinal role of metacognition in reading	Metacognitive knowledge and reading proficiency evolve over time, showing a reciprocal relationship. Improvements in metacognitive knowledge lead to better reading comprehension. The study supports the cyclical development of these skills, emphasising the need to nurture metacognitive awareness for long-term reading comprehension improvement.	F. Teng and Zhang (2021)
Strategy use and proficiency	Successful and unsuccessful EFL students use distinct strategies. Strategy use varies with language proficiency and task requirements. Higher proficiency learners are more aware of and use reading strategies more effectively.	Zhang et al. (2008)

Table 1 (cont.)

Aspect	Key understanding	References
Classification of EFL learners' metacognitive knowledge	Classification of EFL learners' metacognitive knowledge into person, task, and strategy categories. Higher reading scores correlated with greater awareness of reading strategies, particularly comprehension monitoring. Metacognition encompasses knowledge and regulatory skills essential for reading comprehension.	Zhang (2001)
Metacognition and reading proficiency	Metacognitive instruction improved reading comprehension in Hong Kong fifth graders. The study involved stages of reading, reflection, and discussion, leading to higher comprehension scores compared to a control group. Metacognitive knowledge helps learners adapt strategies effectively.	F. Teng (2020a)

Metacognition in Language Teaching 29

However, teachers in classroom settings are often ill equipped to impart such strategies to students. The goal of strategy instruction is to gradually transfer responsibility for selecting, applying, monitoring, and evaluating strategy use from teachers to students. Classroom teachers' under-preparedness to fulfil this objective hampers metacognitive strategy implementation and undermines students' potential to become independent, proficient readers.

3.2.2 When to Facilitate Metacognitive Instruction for Reading?

Metacognitive knowledge heavily contributes to the longitudinal development of young learners' reading and writing skills (F. Teng & Zhang, 2021). While children rely on rehearsal strategies in the early stages of reading, by fourth grade, they become more capable of actively managing their reading and adopting complex cognitive strategies if given strategy instruction (Baker, 2015). F. Teng (2020a) lent support to these findings, documenting that young learners move from an initial reliance on reading and completing exercises to being aware of a wider repertoire of factors influencing their reading. F. Teng (2020a) particularly focused on fifth-grade learners in Hong Kong.

An important consideration in metacognitive instruction for reading is the age at which it should be introduced and how it should be implemented. Metacognitive accuracy may vary with age: younger adults tend to have higher metacognitive accuracy in assessing their cognitive capacity, whereas older adults excel in evaluating their ability to selectively remember information (Urban et al., 2023). This discrepancy suggests there may be separate metacognitive mechanisms which aging differentially affects.

Some people need to devote more cognitive effort to specific tasks as they age, and their cognitive resources may deplete more quickly while doing so. Older adults might then become more discerning when choosing tasks that warrant cognitive resources; this deliberation can be seen as an adaptive response to the reduced cognitive resources available for reading. To explore age-related differences in metacognitive processes, it is advisable to gather evidence on reading strategies' efficacy among young and adult EFL learners by examining the techniques that these groups employ. Creative methods (e.g., reading and writing workshops, reflections, group discussions, and metacognitive strategy instruction) can also be compared.

3.2.3 How to Facilitate Metacognitive Instruction for Reading?

Another crucial aspect is how to facilitate metacognitive instruction for reading. Several factors need to be addressed, including the training sequencing and duration, task selection for teaching and training, instructional delivery (e.g., chosen models), and applicable transfer tasks and assessments (Azevedo, 2020). The sequencing of training refers to the order in which metacognitive knowledge and skills for reading are taught. A sequence may begin with declarative knowledge (i.e., about strategies and processes), followed by procedural knowledge (i.e., about how to use strategies) and then conditional knowledge (i.e., about when and why to use them). This structure allows learners to develop a solid foundation of metacognitive awareness in reading. The length of training regimens is another consideration. Declarative knowledge typically develops more quickly than procedural or conditional knowledge; therefore, the time required to master each form of knowledge may vary.

Learners need sufficient time and practice to internalise metacognitive strategies and apply them effectively. Task selection is also central to teaching and training. Teachers must decide whether to use the same tasks for a specific topic or in different domains. Relatedly, teachers may consider using isomorphic tasks that share underlying structures across topics or domains. Selecting suitable tasks helps build metacognitive awareness and facilitates skill transfer to various reading contexts. The question of who or what should deliver reading instruction and training is important to ponder, too. Options include teachers, parents, peers, experts, or even artificial agents such as virtual humans or robots. The optimal approach might involve a combination of human and artificial agents, leveraging the unique strengths of each to enhance metacognitive instruction. The chosen instructional model will ultimately guide training. The method could entail expert modelling while students engage in vicarious learning, followed by practice using acquired metacognitive knowledge with adaptive scaffolding from experts. Once mastery is demonstrated, scaffolding can gradually decrease, such that learners slowly begin to use metacognitive strategies independently. This cycle can then be repeated for subsequent reading areas to foster domain-general and domain-specific metacognitive skills. New transfer tasks and assessments need to be developed to monitor learners' acquisition, internalisation, retention, retrieval, use, and transfer of metacognitive knowledge for reading comprehension. These tasks should measure learners' ability to deploy metacognitive strategies in different reading contexts in addition to tracking overall metacognitive awareness.

3.3 Summary

This section highlights the role of metacognitive strategic knowledge in promoting individuals' awareness of their learning processes. Encouraging EFL readers to reflect on their own reading processes enables these individuals to use strategic knowledge that enhances their reading effectiveness. Teachers need to support students in applying effective strategies; doing so is key to improving students' reading comprehension. Therefore, metacognition should be part of reading instruction.

Teachers implement numerous instructional methods, such as reflection, modelling, reading and writing workshops, and integrated activity sequences (e.g., reporting and discussing thought processes). These approaches typically focus on both the text and the reading process. They are meant to help readers become more aware of major aspects of the reading process, hone a range of reading-related skills, and ensure that metacognitive instruction in reading remains dynamic and innovative. Learners naturally benefit from being able to critically evaluate text-based content and judge its value.

A combination of methods can facilitate students' independent exploration of content knowledge and their capacity to overcome challenges while reading. Approaches may include reading and writing workshops, reflective activities, group discussions, and metacognitive strategy instruction. These opportunities will empower students to engage with text, ultimately improving learners' comprehension and problem solving.

4 Metacognition in Writing

Metacognition is clearly important in the writing context (Graham et al., 2018; Harris et al., 2009; F. Teng, 2020b; F. Teng & Huang, 2019). Hacker et al. (2009) even described writing as 'applied metacognition' (p. 160), highlighting the connection between writing and metacognitive processes. As mentioned in Section 3, metacognition is composed of two sub-components (i.e., knowledge and regulation). The two sub-components are crucial for the writing process. The knowledge component serves as the basis for student writers' decisions about how to approach a writing task. The regulation component enables them to consciously control the writing process by effectively managing their cognitive load and employing relevant regulation strategies (Harris et al., 2009). Planning, monitoring, and evaluation processes have been identified as key regulation components during writing that greatly influence students' subprocesses (e.g., Bereiter & Scardamalia, 1987; Flower & Hayes, 1981; Hayes, 1996; Kellogg, 1996). These findings provide evidence of metacognition's integral role in writing. This section offers a comprehensive synthesis of the role that metacognition plays in the writing process.

4.1 Understanding Metacognition in Writing

Research on metacognition in the writing context can be categorised into two primary lines of inquiry. The first agenda focuses on metacognitive strategies' predictive impacts on writing. The second concerns how metacognitive training affects writing performance.

Scholars have scrutinised the impacts of various metacognitive strategies on writing performance, with Sophie Lin Teng contributing generously in this regard. One of her highly cited studies (L. Teng & Zhang, 2016) involved 790 undergraduate students from 6 universities in northeastern China. Findings revealed that six out of nine SRL strategies significantly predicted EFL writing proficiency: text processing, idea planning, goal-oriented monitoring and evaluating, feedback handling, emotional control, and motivational self-talk. In another study, L. Teng and Zhang (2018) examined the predictive effects of motivational regulation strategies on EFL students' writing performance, mediated by SRL strategies. The sample included 512 undergraduate students in mainland China. Structural equation modelling confirmed a partial mediating effect, such that motivational regulation strategies influenced participants' writing performance both directly and indirectly. These strategies also significantly correlated with students' reported use of SRL strategies related to cognition, metacognition, and social behaviour. However, only cognitive and metacognitive strategies were significant mediators in this model; social-behavioural strategies were not. L. Teng et al. (2020) used mixed methods to investigate the relationship between writing proficiency levels and motivational regulation strategies in an EFL context. They specifically evaluated 389 Chinese undergraduates' writing proficiency and responses to a self-report questionnaire. Results indicated that participants with high levels of writing proficiency reported greater usage of mastery and performance self-talk, interest enhancement, and emotional control compared with students who displayed low writing proficiency. This discrepancy suggests that intrinsic motivational regulation strategies positively correlate with writing proficiency levels. Qualitative data have supported this conjecture, showing that these strategies can help high-proficiency students develop a sense of achievement, sustain their learning efforts, and cultivate a passion for English-language writing. Sun et al. (2023) also used a mixed-methods approach to investigate the relationship between EFL learners' metacognitive experiences in learning to write and their writing proficiency. Four hundred and forty-nine second-year undergraduates were invited to complete a self-report questionnaire and a writing task. From these participants, ten students were invited to complete follow-up interviews. Quantitative and qualitative findings showed that students at different writing proficiency levels differed in the richness of their metacognitive experiences in writing.

In recent years, L. Teng (2024) explored individual differences in motivational beliefs, self-efficacy, and SRL strategies in writing. A total of 389

Metacognition in Language Teaching   33

learners completed questionnaires covering several factors: motivational beliefs (extrinsic and intrinsic goal orientation, task value, and control of learning belief); self-efficacy (linguistic self-efficacy, performance self-efficacy, and self-regulatory efficacy); and SRL strategies (cognition, metacognition, social behaviour, and motivational regulation). Multiple regression analyses revealed that motivational beliefs forecasted SRL strategies. In particular, task value and intrinsic goal orientation were significant predictors of nine sub-factors of SRL strategies. Self-efficacy emerged as a strong predictor of metacognitive, cognitive, and motivational regulation strategies. Basically, the more positively students view their self-efficacy for completing tasks, the more committed they are to using various strategies to alleviate cognitive burdens and regulate their emotions to sustain learning efforts.

Mark Teng's studies have offered valuable insights into the role of metacognitive strategies in writing. F. Teng and Huang (2019) applied L. Teng and Zhang's (2016) SRL writing strategies in a Chinese secondary school setting with 682 students. The purposes were to identify the roles of self-regulated writing strategies in EFL students' writing proficiency and to determine whether strategy use varied across students. Participants' self-regulated writing strategies indeed influenced writing performance. These results supported the validity of a higher-order self-regulation model that focuses on cognition, metacognition, social behaviour, and motivational regulation (e.g., see Zimmerman, 2011). In line with Kizilcec et al. (2017), students' personal differences affected their SRL strategy use. For example, age, gender, English learning experience, time commitment to writing, familiarity with writing topics, examination experience, school prestige, and interest in learning English all played a part in students' reported use of self-regulated writing strategies.

F. Teng (2020e) also emphasised that metacognitive regulation – encompassing the self-regulatory skills of planning, monitoring, and evaluating – is more crucial for writing performance than metacognitive knowledge. Learners with stronger regulatory skills or higher levels of metacognitive awareness should thus be better at establishing reasonable writing goals and selecting suitable writing strategies, which will significantly enhance their writing performance. In a separate study, F. Teng et al. (2022) validated metacognitive academic writing strategies and evaluated their predictive effects on academic writing performance in a foreign language context. The results supported the anticipated impacts of eight aspects: declarative knowledge, procedural knowledge, conditional knowledge, planning, monitoring, evaluating, information management, and debugging. These strategies were interpreted with reference to the two core paradigms of metacognition – metacognitive knowledge and regulation – as conceptualised by Flavell (1979). Further extending this research, F. Teng et al. (2022) assessed self-regulatory writing strategies among young EFL learners. The authors identified six strategy-related factors – writing planning, goal-oriented monitoring, goal-oriented evaluation, emotional control, memorisation, and metacognitive judgement – that had significant predictive effects on secondary school students' writing performance. Additionally, F. Teng and Yue (2023) highlighted the predictive impacts of metacognitive strategies on academic writing (i.e., declarative, procedural, and conditional knowledge as well as planning, monitoring, evaluating, information management, and debugging). They also discerned correlations between metacognition, critical thinking skills, and academic writing, underscoring metacognitive strategies' comprehensive impact on writing performance.

Four other pieces of research have recently reinforced the predictive effects of metacognition in writing. F. Teng and Qin (2024) observed that eight types of metacognitive writing strategies – motivation and interest, debugging strategies, declarative knowledge, procedural knowledge, text-processing skills, planning, monitoring, and evaluating – significantly predicted learners' writing performance in a multimedia environment. F. Teng and Ma (2024) assessed metacognition-based feedback literacy; their study was the first to evaluate student feedback literacy from a metacognitive perspective. Results indicated that feedback-related strategies, including participation, motivation, feedback-related monitoring techniques, and strategy knowledge, had predictive effects on EFL learners' academic writing performance. F. Teng and Zhang (2024b) conducted a pair of studies within a multimedia writing environment: the first study validated L2 self-regulated strategies in writing; the second demonstrated the predictive effects of self-regulated strategies, working memory, and L2 proficiency on L2 writing performance. Lastly, Shen and F. Teng (2024) explored artificial intelligence (AI)-assisted writing, a contemporary topic given the prevalence of AI. Their findings supported the predictive effects of self-directed learning competency on AI-assisted writing and highlighted its correlation with learners' critical thinking skills. These recent studies collectively underscore the significance of metacognitive strategies in enhancing writing performance across diverse contexts and modalities, from multimedia environments to AI-assisted writing.

Table 2 presents the synthesised information the predictive effects of metacognitive strategies in writing.

The reviewed body of research provides a holistic picture of how metacognitive and SRL strategies affect EFL students' writing performance, illuminating the intricate relationship between metacognitive strategies and writing proficiency. Scholars have adopted robust methods and offered actionable

Table 2 Predictive effects of metacognitive strategies in writing

Study	Participants & setting	Methodology	Key findings
L. Teng & Zhang (2016)	790 undergraduate students from six universities in northeastern China	Analysis of SRL strategies predicting EFL writing proficiency	Six SRL strategies (text processing, idea planning, goal-oriented monitoring and evaluating, feedback handling, emotional control, motivational self-talk) significantly predicted writing proficiency.
L. Teng & Zhang (2018)	512 undergraduate students in mainland China	Structural equation modelling to examine motivational regulation strategies' effects	Motivational regulation strategies influenced writing performance directly and indirectly via SRL strategies. Cognitive and metacognitive strategies were significant mediators, while social-behavioural strategies were not.
L. Teng et al. (2020)	389 Chinese undergraduates	Mixed methods to assess writing proficiency and motivational regulation strategies	High writing proficiency correlated with greater use of mastery and performance self-talk, interest enhancement, and emotional control. These strategies fostered a sense of achievement and sustained learning efforts in high-proficiency students.

Table 2 (cont.)

Study	Participants & setting	Methodology	Key findings
L. Teng (2024)	389 university students in China	Questionnaires on motivational beliefs, self-efficacy, and SRL strategies	Motivational beliefs predicted SRL strategies, with task value and intrinsic goal orientation as significant predictors. Self-efficacy strongly predicted metacognitive, cognitive, and motivational regulation strategies.
F. Teng & Huang (2019)	682 Chinese secondary school students	Application of L. Teng & Zhang's (2016) SRL writing strategies	Self-regulated writing strategies influenced writing performance. Strategy use varied across students due to personal differences like age, gender, English learning experience, and interest in learning English.
F. Teng (2020e)	882 Chinese university students	Questionnaire on metacognition and a writing test	Metacognitive regulation (planning, monitoring, evaluating) is crucial for writing performance. Strong regulatory skills enhance goal-setting and strategy selection, improving writing outcomes.
F. Teng, Qin, & Wang (2022)	664 Chinese university students	Validation of metacognitive academic writing strategies through SEM	Eight strategies (declarative knowledge, procedural knowledge, conditional knowledge, planning, monitoring, evaluating, information management, debugging) predicted academic writing performance.

F. Teng et al. (2022)	Two samples of 669 and 239 secondary school students	Assessment of self-regulatory writing strategies through EFA and CFA	Six strategy-related factors (writing planning, goal-oriented monitoring, goal-oriented evaluation, emotional control, memorisation, metacognitive judgement) significantly predicted writing performance.
F. Teng & Yue (2023)	644 Chinese university students	Examination of metacognitive strategies on academic writing	Metacognitive strategies (declarative, procedural, conditional knowledge, planning, monitoring, evaluating, information management, debugging) predicted academic writing performance, correlating with critical thinking skills.
F. Teng & Qin (2024)	957 Chinese university students	Validation of metacognitive writing strategies in a multimedia environment	Eight metacognitive strategies (motivation and interest, debugging, declarative knowledge, procedural knowledge, text-processing, planning, monitoring, evaluating) predicted writing performance.
F. Teng & Ma (2024)	708 Chinese university students	Assessment of metacognition-based feedback literacy	Feedback-related strategies (participation, motivation, monitoring, strategy knowledge) predicted academic writing performance.
F. Teng & Zhang (2024b)	Two samples of 400 and 406 Chinese university students	Validation of L2 self-regulated strategies in a multimedia writing environment	Self-regulated strategies, working memory, and L2 proficiency predicted L2 writing performance

implications for educators, richly contributing to cognitive writing models. However, authors have predominantly used Chinese EFL student samples; this condition raises questions about findings' applicability in other cultural and linguistic contexts. The long-term impacts of these strategies are also unclear, necessitating longitudinal studies to track sustained effects. Furthermore, although these studies have acknowledged the complexity of metacognitive knowledge, none explored how associated nuances inform writing outcomes. The interaction effects between strategies and individual differences also have yet to be thoroughly examined, and qualitative insights are not as prominent as quantitative ones. Given these constraints, more studies are needed to understand the roles of metacognitive and SRL strategies in enhancing writing performance. Related work will deepen the understanding of how best to support student writers.

The second issue relates to training-oriented interventions, which aim to equip students with the knowledge and skills required to reflect on and regulate their writing processes effectively (e.g., Nguyen & Gu, 2013; F. Teng, 2016). Metacognitive training interventions often involve explicit instruction on metacognitive strategies, such as planning, monitoring, and evaluating one's writing. Studies have shown promising results overall, indicating that metacognitive training can improve various aspects of writing (e.g., content organisation, idea generation, revision skills, and general writing quality). By cultivating metacognitive awareness and providing students with strategies to regulate their writing, interventions on fostering metacognitive awareness empower learners to become more autonomous, reflective, and effective writers.

An illustrative study by Larkin (2009) delved into this topic by investigating how metacognitive instruction affected the writing abilities of 172 sixth-grade students attending 5 primary schools in England. Taking a qualitative approach, Larkin (2009) observed twenty-five writing lessons and documented her interpretations of each. Data collection consisted of roughly twenty-five hours of video-based observations along with analyses of teachers' reflections and notes. Findings showed that young learners were able to engage in metacognitive talk and purposefully employ metacognitive strategies while co-constructing written texts. Through metacognitive instruction, students developed the capacity to reflect on their writing, monitor their progress, and make intentional decisions to enhance the quality of their written work. The study provided valuable information about metacognitive instruction's potential to empower young learners to actively deploy metacognitive processes while writing.

Nguyen and Gu (2013) conducted a mixed-method study to inspect the impact of metacognitive strategy training on writing performance among 130 third-year English majors in a Vietnamese EFL setting. The researchers created a nine-lesson metacognitive strategy training programme, which covered components such as planning, monitoring, and evaluating in the context of writing. Participants were separated into three groups: one group received strategy-based instruction, and the other two groups served as controls. The participants who received metacognitive strategy instruction demonstrated significantly improved writing performance compared with their control-group counterparts. Specifically, students who completed metacognitive training were more skilled at planning, monitoring, and evaluating their writing tasks. Group interviews were held immediately after the training with several participants from the experimental group. All five students reported changes in their approach to writing tasks since receiving metacognitive training. They stated that they thought more deliberately prior to writing, paid greater attention to their essays' content, and actively searched for relevant information on the given topic. Moreover, one student remarked that she had learnt effective techniques for organising her essay, indicating progress in the structural dimension of her writing.

Mark Teng has conducted extensive research on using cooperative metacognitive training to enhance university students' writing. F. Teng's (2016) study involved 120 university students who were exposed to 1 of 3 conditions: a cooperative learning condition with embedded metacognitive instruction (COOP + META), a cooperative learning condition (COOP), and a no-treatment control group. Quantitative analysis revealed that participants in the COOP + META group achieved the highest mean scores on a compare-and-contrast essay, followed by participants in the COOP condition and the control group. Including metacognitive instruction within a cooperative learning environment thus positively influenced students' writing performance. In addition, this study's qualitative findings shed light on the strategies that participants in the COOP + META group used to regulate their cognitive processes while writing. These techniques consisted of engaging in reflective thinking before writing, planning the written content, better organising the content, monitoring their progress, choosing appropriate writing strategies, assessing their written work, and making meaningful connections while writing. Notably, students in the COOP+META group planned, monitored, and evaluated their writing process more frequently than the other groups. These inclinations imply that this group's metacognitive training helped them engage in metacognitive processes and effectively regulate their writing.

In another study, F. Teng (2020b) assigned 120 university students into three groups: group feedback guidance (GFG), self-explanation guidance (SEG), and a control group (CG). Learners in the GFG and SEG groups both received metacognitive instruction; however, learners in the GFG condition focused on providing and receiving feedback in writing, whereas learners in the SEG focused on self-constructing explanations or arguments. Ultimately, the GFG group outperformed the SEG and CG groups in terms of English writing as measured by an immediate and delayed writing test. An analysis of the groups' journal entries indicated that participants in the GFG group displayed better awareness of writing task perception and stronger self-regulation of writing. These students also applied metacognitive strategies more often than their peers in the other groups.

F. Teng (2020c) investigated how collaborative writing supported by interactive whiteboard technology could affect students' writing performance. The study centred on 120 university EFL students. Quantitative results showed that integrating this technology with collaborative writing instruction led to the greatest improvement in students' writing performance, followed by traditional whiteboard-integrated collaborative writing and, lastly, traditional collaborative writing instruction without whiteboard technology. Qualitative results indicated that the patterns and timing of metacognitive activities varied across the three groups. Learners who received interactive whiteboard–integrated collaborative writing instruction displayed higher levels of metacognitive activities and were more engaged in co-regulation than other groups. The interactive whiteboard condition facilitated participants' adoption of writing strategies that promoted emerging cognitive functions and timely execution of routines during collaborative writing. Team members pooled their linguistic knowledge, tracked the writing process, and decided on strategies or corrective feedback to align their efforts and produce the intended writing output. Consequently, learners created significantly better written products.

F. Teng (2021a) explored the potential effectiveness of incorporating metacognitive prompts, a form of metacognitive guidance, into collaborative writing to enhance academic English writing skills. A set of 160 university students was divided into 4 instructional groups: collaborative writing with embedded metacognitive guidance, metacognitive training without collaborative writing, collaborative writing without metacognitive training, and individual learning. Four test components were considered: reproduction of text structure knowledge, application of text structure knowledge, reduction of text content, and abstract writing. Findings highlighted the importance of introducing metacognitive strategies into collaborative writing to develop university EFL students' academic writing abilities. Metacognitive prompts in collaborative writing enhanced participants' skills in using prompts to share knowledge, transform their knowledge for academic communication, and apply their knowledge to benefit peers. This process also facilitated learners' coordination in planning ideas, generating text, and reviewing ideas and text. Acquiring academic writing skills involves both observation and practice – both of which improved participants' academic writing skills in this case.

F. Teng (2022a) examined the effects of cooperative metacognitive instruction on university EFL learners' writing skills and metacognitive awareness. The study involved three groups: a cooperative learning group with metacognitive instruction (EG), a metacognitive instruction-only group, and a cooperative learning-only group. The EG students outperformed the others in academic writing as well as metacognitive regulation. Participants whose metacognitive regulation did not improve were less likely to show significantly enhanced writing skills. Learners who received cooperative metacognitive instruction were better equipped to improve their writing performance compared with those who studied in cooperative settings without metacognitive interventions or those who received metacognitive instruction without cooperative learning. Similar results were reported by Teng (2022b), such that learners exposed to metacognitive prompts in a cooperative learning setting performed best in metacognitive awareness and EFL writing.

F. Teng and Huang (2023) tested four instructional approaches – metacognitive instruction in a collaborative writing setting, metacognitive instruction in an individual setting, collaborative writing, and individual writing – with a sample of 352 Chinese university EFL students. Combining metacognitive instruction and collaborative writing promoted writing accuracy but neither fluency nor complexity. One explanation for this finding is that blending metacognitive prompts into a collaborative writing setting afforded the participants more opportunities to engage with different aspects of writing while composing essays together. However, none of the four conditions simultaneously increased accuracy, fluency, and complexity. The retrieval of lexical complexity may have interfered, as finding precise words can reduce fluency. Focusing on clauses' accuracy could also compromise their complexity. Developing writing complexity, accuracy, and fluency concurrently might have been particularly challenging for Chinese university EFL learners. It is therefore important to acknowledge the assumed competition for attentional resources when writing.

Researchers have also considered training young students' self-regulated strategies for writing. For example, F. Teng (2019) looked into how text structure and self-regulated strategies affect young ESL learners' writing quality in Hong Kong. The following three conditions applied: text structure instruction (TSI), self-regulated strategy instruction (SRSI), and a CG. Each consisted of twenty one-hour sessions, with measures including a written summary and an essay. Ultimately, compared with traditional instruction, the TSI and SRSI groups exhibited better writing outcomes. Teaching self-regulated strategies indeed improved participants' writing quality, and teaching about text structure enhanced their capacity to summarise main ideas.

In another study (F. Teng, 2020d), 144 Chinese primary school students were divided into four groups: self-regulated strategy development + collaborative modelling of text structure, collaborative modelling of text structure only, self-regulated strategy development only, and traditional instruction. Outcome measures included content comprehension, summarisation of main ideas, and essay writing. The combination of self-regulated strategy development and collaborative modelling of text structure was found to be particularly useful for increasing students' content comprehension and writing quality. These results suggest that writing is a complex process requiring students to master task-specific strategies and develop metacognitive awareness for regulating and controlling strategy use.

F. Teng (2021b) later performed research in which 178 primary school students were separated into four groups: text structure instruction + self-regulation strategy development (TSI + SRSD), TSI only, SRSD only, and a CG. The aim was to investigate potential improvements in summarising main ideas and essay writing following the intervention. The TSI + SRSD intervention was especially effective in enhancing participants' abilities to summarise main ideas and compose essays. Integrating TSI with SRSD instruction may enable learners to generate more ideas in their writing, plan more elaborately, and produce syntactically accurate sentences. Thus, intensive training in text structure knowledge may be necessary for primary school students to fully benefit from SRSD interventions. This finding signals that multicomponent interventions geared towards core writing processes (e.g., metacognition, self-regulation, and text structure) could be helpful for young student writers.

L. Teng and Zhang (2020) conducted a five-month study administering SRL strategy-based instruction to one group of students while a CG received a standard academic writing course for the same duration. Participants completed pre-, post-, and delayed post-writing tests along with self-report questionnaires at the beginning and end of the intervention. Results demonstrated that the intervention group significantly outperformed the CG on the post- and delayed post-writing tests. Students in the intervention group became more proactive in employing a variety of SRL strategies, including metacognitive strategies, social-behavioural strategies, and motivational regulation strategies. They also demonstrated greater tendencies to consider key elements of effective composition and to monitor their knowledge mastery in relation to specific learning goals. Furthermore, they explored different methods to engage more enthusiastically with writing tasks. The intervention also enhanced participants' self-efficacy in using linguistic knowledge to construct written texts.

Table 3 presents synthesised information on metacognitive training for writing

Table 3 Intervention of metacognitive training for writing

Study	Participants & setting	Methodology	Key findings
Larkin (2009)	172 sixth-grade students in five primary schools in England	Qualitative study with 25 writing lessons observed, 25 hours of video-based observations, teacher reflections	Students engaged in metacognitive talk and strategies, enhancing their ability to reflect, monitor, and improve their writing through metacognitive instruction.
Nguyen and Gu (2013)	130 third-year English majors in a Vietnamese EFL setting	Mixed-method study with a nine-lesson metacognitive strategy training program	Students receiving metacognitive strategy instruction showed improved writing performance, particularly in planning, monitoring, and evaluating writing tasks. Participants reported deliberate thinking and better content attention.
F. Teng (2016)	120 university students	Cooperative learning with embedded metacognitive instruction (COOP + META), COOP,. and control group	COOP + META group achieved highest essay scores. Metacognitive instruction in cooperative settings enhanced reflective thinking, planning, monitoring, and evaluating writing processes.

Table 3 (cont.)

Study	Participants & setting	Methodology	Key findings
F. Teng (2020b)	120 university students in China	Group feedback guidance (GFG), self-explanation guidance (SEG), and control group	GFG group outperformed others in writing tests. Participants showed better task perception and self-regulation, using metacognitive strategies more frequently.
F. Teng (2020c)	120 Chinese university EFL students	Collaborative writing with interactive whiteboard technology	Interactive whiteboard condition led to greatest writing improvement. Students engaged in higher metacognitive activities and co-regulation, improving writing strategy adoption.
F. Teng (2020d)	144 Chinese primary school students	Self-regulated strategy development + collaborative modelling of text structure	Combination of strategies improved content comprehension and writing quality. Mastery of task-specific strategies and metacognitive awareness was crucial for writing improvement.
F. Teng (2021a)	160 university students in China	Collaborative writing with metacognitive guidance	Metacognitive prompts in collaborative writing enhanced academic writing skills, coordination, and knowledge transformation.
F. Teng (2021b)	178 primary school students in China	Text structure instruction + self-regulation strategy development (TSI + SRSD)	TSI + SRSD intervention effectively enhanced summarisation and essay writing skills. Intensive text structure knowledge training was beneficial for young writers.

Study	Participants	Intervention	Key findings
F. Teng (2022a)	University EFL learners in China	Cooperative metacognitive instruction	EG group outperformed others in writing and metacognitive regulation. Cooperative metacognitive instruction improved writing performance and metacognitive awareness.
F. Teng & Huang (2023)	352 Chinese university EFL students	COOP+META, COOP, META, and control group	Combining metacognitive instruction with collaborative writing improved writing accuracy. Challenges in developing accuracy, fluency, and complexity concurrently were noted.
F. Teng (2019)	Young ESL learners in Hong Kong	Text structure instruction (TSI), self-regulated strategy instruction (SRSI), and control group	TSI and SRSI groups showed better writing outcomes. Self-regulated strategies improved writing quality, and text structure instruction enhanced summarisation skills.
L. Teng & Zhang (2020)	80 Chinese university students	SRL strategy-based instruction vs. standard academic writing course; Pre-, post-, and delayed post-writing tests with self-report questionnaires	Intervention group outperformed control group in writing tests. Students became proactive in using SRL strategies, improving self-efficacy and engagement in writing tasks.

The aforementioned studies underscore the effectiveness of metacognitive instruction in enhancing metacognitive skills – particularly metacognitive regulation – and improving writing performance. Writing is a multifaceted socio-cognitive activity for which metacognitive instruction is highly efficacious (Larkin, 2009). The recursive and cognitive nature of writing explains this activity's complexity (Kress, 1982). Research outcomes have substantiated cognitive writing models, such as that by Hayes (1996), who conceptualised writing as a hierarchically and recursively organised process. The Hayes model posits that writing places sizable cognitive demands on working memory, especially when some processes interrupt others. Text generation is viewed as a problem-solving and goal-oriented activity that requires student writers to adjust their objectives as they progress through a task. The complexity of writing also arises from the need to transform ideas into written form, as Scardamalia and Bereiter's (1987) models (i.e., the knowledge-telling model and the knowledge-transforming model) suggest. The knowledge-telling model describes the processes of novice writers, who often work on a composition without goal-directed planning. By contrast, the knowledge-transforming model explains the composition process for mature writers, who can generally control and direct their writing well. Evidence supports the training of students' metacognitive awareness to potentially enhance metacognitive regulation. However, the complexity of metacognitive knowledge is a lingering concern and may partly explain why improvements in metacognitive knowledge are not guaranteed. Another issue is that metacognitive training, despite possibly leading to enhanced metacognitive regulation and improved writing, may not always result in immediate or observable gains in metacognitive knowledge itself. Metacognitive regulation undoubtedly plays a part in writing. Learning to write coherent, effective texts represents a long-time achievement in cognitive development and is decidedly different from speech acquisition. The basic writing processes – planning, language generation, and reviewing – and the mental representations that must be generated and maintained in working memory undergo developmental changes through maturation and learning within specific writing tasks (Kellogg, 2008). Therefore, the complexity of writing as a cognitive process necessitates a thoughtful, sustained approach to metacognitive training.

4.2 Critical Issues

4.2.1 To What Extent Do Metacognitive Strategies Predict Writing?

A critical issue in writing-related research is determining the extent to which metacognitive strategies predict writing performance. The above-mentioned

Metacognition in Language Teaching 47

studies largely focused on strategies associated with metacognitive knowledge and regulation. However, these strategies' definitions may have overlap, which could confuse readers. For instance, even though techniques like planning, monitoring, and evaluating are routinely discussed, their applications can vary. Some scholars might categorise text-processing skills under metacognitive regulation, while others consider these capacities part of procedural knowledge. This inconsistency in terminology and classification can make it challenging to draw conclusions about each strategy's contributions.

Moreover, although the predictive effects of metacognitive strategies are well-documented, the mechanisms through which these strategies influence writing performance are not always clearly articulated. For example, how do strategies like motivational self-talk and emotional control specifically enhance the writing process? What roles do feedback-related strategies play in fostering better writing outcomes? Another point of deliberation is the context in which these strategies are used. Research involving multimedia environments, traditional classroom settings, and AI-assisted writing platforms may yield distinct insights into the effectiveness of metacognitive strategies. These techniques' transferability across learning situations continues to merit exploration. More longitudinal studies are also needed to track how metacognitive strategy instruction affects writing performance in the long term. Most studies have concentrated on short-term interventions and their immediate effects, leaving a gap in our comprehension of how these strategies influence writing development over time.

The final concern is the reliance on self-report data to assess metacognitive strategy use. Self-report measures can be subjective and may not actually reflect learners' behaviours or cognitive processes. Students might overestimate or underestimate their use of metacognitive strategies due to social desirability bias, limited self-awareness, or misconstrued survey items. These possibilities cast doubt on findings' validity and whether self-report instruments truly capture respondents' experiences.

4.2.2 To What Extent Is Metacognitive Training Effective for Writing?

Another core issue is determining the extent to which metacognitive training helps improve writing skills. Research has revealed numerous positive effects of metacognitive training on writing performance; however, several uncertainties remain, particularly regarding how best to apply these findings in diverse classroom settings. Much of the intervention research conducted thus far has included specific, often brief training periods. These studies typically measure immediate or short-term gains in writing performance, leaving ambiguities about the long-term sustainability of the benefits derived from metacognitive training. Without longitudinal data, it is difficult to ascertain whether the improvements seen in these studies will endure over time or wane once the training period concludes.

Another point of interest is participant homogeneity. Most samples contained individuals with similar proficiency – usually higher than the intermediate level. It is therefore unclear whether the results are generalisable to a range of learners, particularly those at lower proficiency levels. It is similarly uncertain whether the metacognitive strategies that are effective for intermediate or advanced learners will be equally beneficial for beginners or for students struggling with foundational writing skills.

Furthermore, the controlled environments in which these studies have been performed may not accurately reflect the complexities of real-world settings. In classroom teaching, educators encounter myriad student needs, levels of motivation, and learning contexts, all of which can inform the effectiveness of metacognitive training. The structured and often ideal conditions in research studies may not capture the unpredictability of real teaching. Scholars still need to explore how metacognitive training can be brought into existing curricula and teaching practices. Teachers may require targeted training and resources to successfully implement metacognitive strategies in their classrooms. The scalability of such interventions and their adaptability to various educational contexts warrant further investigation.

The final factor that impacts the reliability of findings in the role of metacognitive training on writing could be the diversified test on writing. This means that the way writing ability is assessed can significantly influence the outcomes of studies on metacognitive training. Diversified testing involves using a variety of assessment types and formats to evaluate writing skills, which can include timed essays, reflective journals, research papers, and creative writing tasks, among others.

4.3 Summary

Writing is a developmental process that begins with simply recording thoughts retrieved from long-term memory before evolving into the more complicated task of transforming these thoughts and ideas into a new knowledge structure. Student writers must employ various metacognitive strategies to achieve their writing goals. For instance, planning, evaluating, problem solving, and revising are essential aspects of writing performance. Effective metacognitive training can encompass several key features: (a) facilitating self-planning, self-monitoring, and self-evaluation of the writing process; (b) providing instruction on specific drafting, editing, and revising strategies; and (c) adopting a dialogic approach to presenting and modelling text structure knowledge.

5 Metacognition in Listening

Listening poses great challenges for L2 and FL learners due to constraints in these students' abilities to recognise words in streams of speech and apply corresponding knowledge (Goh, 2023). These struggles are partly attributable to the unidirectionality and intangible nature of the listening process (Goh, 2000; Vandergrift, 2007). This complexity likely contributes to why listening is the least studied language skill compared to reading and writing, as it involves implicit processes that are difficult to access (Vandergrift, 2007).

Metacognition, which encompasses learners' knowledge about and regulation of their cognitive activities during the learning process (Flavell, 1979), is crucial for L2 listening. Metacognitive awareness can be linked to 'listener awareness of the cognitive processes involved in comprehension and the capacity to oversee, regulate, and direct these processes' (Vandergrift & Baker, 2018, p. 85). Low-proficiency students have been shown to complete more diligent self-regulated listening practice outside the classroom compared with their highly proficient peers (Zhou & Rose, 2024). Despite evidence supporting the roles of metacognitive awareness and strategies in enhancing learners' listening proficiency, the relationship between these factors remains inconclusive. This section draws a picture on depicting the role of metacognitive awareness in listening.

5.1 Understanding Metacognition in Listening

Several theories have outlined methods for incorporating metacognitive instruction into listening comprehension. For example, Vandergrift (2004) proposed a metacognitive cycle designed to help learners systematically apply metacognitive strategies while listening. This cycle consists of five stages: planning/predicting, first verification, second verification, final verification, and reflection.

Planning/Predicting: In this stage, students familiarise themselves with the topic and text type. They also predict the kinds of information and words they might hear. Metacognitive strategies employed here include planning and directed attention.

First Verification: During this stage, students verify their initial hypotheses, rectify any inaccuracies, and note additional information. The strategies used include monitoring, planning, and selective attention.

Second Verification: In this stage, students address points of disagreement, make necessary corrections, and grasp finer details. This stage often involves class discussions and reflections to help students understand the meanings of specific words or parts of the text. Relevant metacognitive strategies are monitoring, problem solving, and evaluation.

Final Verification: Here, students listen for information they could not decipher during earlier stages or class discussions. The strategies applied include selective attention and monitoring.

Reflection: In the final stage, learners adopt strategies to compensate for misunderstandings and set goals for future listening activities. The primary metacognitive strategy in this phase is evaluation.

By following this metacognitive cycle, learners can systematically develop their listening comprehension skills through the structured application of and reflection on various metacognitive strategies. Vandergrift's metacognitive cycle provides a framework that enhances listening skills and fosters a deeper understanding of metacognitive processes in language learning. Taken together, these five stages offer insights into how metacognition is conceptualised in listening. By breaking down the listening process into stages, learners can better see how to actively engage with and manage their cognitive processes. This approach helps learners become more aware of their listening strategies and how to regulate them. It also highlights the importance of continuous reflection and adjustment, enabling learners to develop a more adaptable approach to listening comprehension.

Goh (2008) identified two types of learning activities for listening based on the key principles for successful metacognitive instruction that Veenman, Van Hout-Wolters, and Afflerbach (2006) outlined. The first type, integrated experiential listening tasks, enables learners to engage in the social-cognitive processes of listening comprehension. Students primarily use course books or teacher-prepared materials. The focus is on extracting information and constructing meaning. By merging listening activities with metacognitive prompts, learners can become aware of the numerous cognitive processes that L2 listening entails. Students can then apply metacognitive knowledge to their listening development outside the classroom, explore their self-concept as listeners, use appropriate strategies while listening, and identify factors that may influence their listening performance. The second type of activity is guided reflections for listening. It aims to elicit learners' implicit knowledge about L2 listening and encourages them to build new knowledge to better understand their listening experiences. Through reflections, learners can recall previous listening events and plot out strategies to manage their learning. Such introspection helps learners analyse their listening processes, recognise successful strategies, and see areas for improvement. Both types of activities have notable implications for conceiving metacognition in relation to listening. Structured tasks and reflective practices can promote learners' awareness and regulation of their cognitive processes. By completing experiential tasks and guided reflections, learners can more readily grasp metacognitive strategies and their utility to become effective, autonomous listeners.

Research has consistently supported the adoption of metacognitive strategies to enhance listening skills. For instance, Goh and Taib (2006) devised a series of eight process-based listening lessons designed for primary school students. These lessons follow a three-stage sequence: listen and answer, reflect, and report and discuss. Goh and Taib's (2006) research indicated that, after finishing the eight lessons, learners exhibited significant improvements in their metacognitive knowledge concerning listening. All students reported a richer understanding of the components needed to increase listening comprehension. They also demonstrated greater confidence when performing listening tasks and used more effective strategic knowledge to overcome challenges in listening comprehension. Weaker students actually received the most substantial benefits from these process-based lessons, signifying the approach's suitability for diverse learning needs. In another study, Vandergrift (2005) focused on fifty-seven French adolescent learners who took a metacognitive awareness listening questionnaire, a motivation questionnaire, and a listening comprehension test. The results revealed a strong correlation between intrinsic motivation and the frequent use of metacognitive listening strategies. Findings further underscored a progressively stronger relationship between students' reported use of metacognitive listening strategies and their levels of self-determined motivation for listening. This pattern implies that intrinsic motivation is vital for applying metacognitive strategies, as more intrinsically driven listeners tend to use these strategies more often and successfully. These two studies jointly demonstrate that metacognition in listening involves an awareness and regulation of one's listening processes as well as the strategic application of this awareness to strengthen comprehension and overcome listening challenges. Intrinsic motivation is hence pivotal to the fruitful implementation of metacognitive strategies: it prompts learners to engage more closely and consistently with these methods.

Vandergriff and Goh (2012) defined metacognition in listening as listeners' awareness of their cognitive processes. The authors' instructional framework for teaching metacognitive skills in listening consists of three components: knowing, sensing, and doing. These elements are operationalised as using prior knowledge (schema), processing information during listening, and employing self-regulating strategies both during and after listening. Peer interaction is crucial throughout the learning process. Vandergriff and Goh's (2012) proposed pedagogical sequence includes planning, goal setting, predicting, monitoring, evaluating, reflecting, and problem solving. They argued that classroom-based metacognitive instruction particularly benefits low-proficiency learners. Students at an early stage of language acquisition should gain the most from a metacognitive approach to listening. Thus, metacognition in listening can be understood as an awareness and regulation of one's cognitive processes, requiring the strategic use of prior knowledge, active processing during listening, and continuous self-regulation to enhance comprehension and problem-solving abilities.

Goh and Vandergrift (2021) later synthesised available research on listening, referring to historical means of listening instruction and identifying these methods' drawbacks. The pitfalls include limited understanding of the listening process itself and an overemphasis on comprehending input as the sole measure of listening skills. The authors instead recommended a learner-centred approach to listening that integrates metacognitive strategies. These techniques are intended to help students understand how they learn, self-correct, and improve their overall listening experience. Goh and Vandergrift's (2021) definition of teaching succinctly captures this approach: 'Teaching is the process by which novices learn a skill or acquire knowledge with the help of expert input, scaffolding, and guidance' (p. 189). Their description emphasises expert support and structured guidance in helping learners develop effective listening skills.

Based on the summarised studies, learners' metacognitive awareness of listening is integral to listening comprehension. Metacognitive instruction is believed to give learners opportunities to develop their listening comprehension skills. However, instruction on metacognitive listening strategies must be tailored to students' needs. A core aspect is fostering students' awareness of self-evaluation: being able to self-evaluate can enhance students' self-efficacy, as their motivation to engage in self-assessment and problem solving arises from instruction regarding metacognitive listening strategies. Scholars have also provided evidence that language educators can design appropriate, evidence-based curricula, particularly for learners with varying levels of language proficiency. Contextual, learner-related, and cultural factors may influence students' knowledge and willingness to adopt metacognitive strategies for achieving L2 listening comprehension. Accordingly, Goh (2018) framed metacognition as involving mental activities such as 'directly attending to input, processing it in working memory, and storing the processed knowledge and understanding in long-term memory for retrieval and use' (p. 1). Yet gaps exist between metacognitive instruction and the processing that is mandatory for L2 listening; to bridge them, metacognitive instruction should stress learners' conscious awareness of their cognitive activities. Students' retrieval of L2 knowledge will then be more accurate and faster, and they will know how to expedite their learning during future tasks (Sato, 2022).

5.2 Critical Issues

5.2.1 The Extent of Metacognitive Facilitation for Listening

One critical issue lies in the extent of metacognitive facilitation for listening. The aforementioned studies encapsulate the significant impact of metacognitive instruction on listening. Importantly, though, listening comprehension transcends auditory perception. It involves a sophisticated set of cognitive abilities with which learners can discern critical information, unravel subtle meanings, and infer context from a diverse array of spoken cues. Its importance is rooted not just in language comprehension but in broader communicative competence and intercultural insight. Thus, EFL students must adeptly engage with the complexities of spoken English. This capacity manifests from several facets: engaging assertively and dynamically in dialogues and discussions, internalising sophisticated vocabulary, grasping complicated syntactic constructions, emulating authentic pronunciation patterns, and understanding the cultural peculiarities of English-speaking communities.

Applying metacognitive strategies for EFL listening instruction signifies an educational shift towards autonomous learning. These strategies involve advanced cognitive skills encompassing self-awareness, regulatory control, and deliberate orchestration of one's learning activities, which jointly contribute to listening performance (Vandergrift & Goh, 2012). While this step is important, the critical issue is not merely instruction-oriented; a key question is how to integrate these strategies to suit specific listening requirements. Each metacognitive strategy should be tailored to the needs of listening tasks. For instance, when highlighting personal knowledge, people must be able to access their pre-existing repository of information, experiences, and convictions through metacognitive knowledge. Despite researchers advocating for metacognitive training, the literature has insufficiently considered how each strategy aligns with listening-related tasks. It is crucial to teach students how to home in on the linguistic elements of spoken English to capture crucial auditory information. Metacognitive strategies thus need to be incorporated into particular listening activities to be effective.

- Accessing Prior Knowledge: Encourage students to draw on their knowledge and experiences before listening to a new piece of audio.
- Monitoring Understanding: Teach students to continually check their comprehension during listening in order to identify and address gaps in understanding.
- Evaluating Performance: Guide students in assessing their listening performance after completing a task (e.g., by reflecting on which strategies worked and which could be improved).

- Planning and Setting Goals: Help students set specific listening goals and plan how to achieve them (e.g., focusing on understanding the main ideas or specific details).

However, metacognitive facilitation for listening can be influenced by several factors, impacting how effectively individuals employ strategies to enhance their listening skills. Learners' prior knowledge and experience play a crucial role, as those with more exposure to the language or specific content may apply metacognitive strategies more effectively (Vandergrift & Goh, 2012). Motivation and attitude are also significant; highly motivated learners are more likely to engage in planning, monitoring, and evaluating their listening processes, leading to better outcomes (Graham, 2006). The cognitive load of listening material can affect facilitation, as overly complex content might overwhelm cognitive resources, hindering strategy application (Sweller, 1988). Instructional support, particularly explicit teaching and modelling of strategies, enhances learners' self-regulation abilities (O'Malley & Chamot, 1990). Environmental factors, such as noise and distractions, can impede concentration and strategy use, making a conducive listening environment essential (Rost, 2016). Finally, individual differences, including age, cognitive abilities, and personality traits, can affect strategy use, with those possessing higher working memory capacity potentially managing strategies more effectively (Baddeley, 2003). Understanding these factors can aid educators in designing effective listening instruction that supports metacognitive strategy development, thereby improving listening comprehension and language proficiency.

5.2.2 Metacognitive Strategies for Listening

Metacognitive strategies are of paramount importance in listening instruction. New information is encountered in the classroom nearly every day. However, students cannot always figure out how new material connects to what has already been covered – or even whether something that they know is important to think about. For many teachers, presenting a new lesson can just feel like adding another disembodied idea or concept to the mix. Students then tend to absorb knowledge passively by taking notes without thinking critically. Even though each new lesson introduces fresh information, if that material seems disjointed from prior learning, it can become overwhelming.

Metacognitive strategies matter for listening because it involves understanding, on a larger scale, how ideas build upon each other. Teachers should realise that an intentional continuum exists, which stretches through units and proficiency levels, linking to existing background knowledge. This approach helps build deeper, more durable knowledge and encourages students to take ownership

Metacognition in Language Teaching 55

of their own learning, especially in listening. Many teachers' instructional practices lack metacognitive awareness. Even teachers who possess some degree of metacognitive awareness often separate metacognitive training from listening instruction. They may focus on instilling in students the metacognitive habits to actively reflect on one's learning process with the aim of developing self-sufficient learners. However, it is equally important to train students to grapple with new material through a reflection on metacognitive strategies. Then they can see how newly introduced information fits into the puzzle of what they already know, solidifies concepts, or reveals gaps in their knowledge.

To help students build the metacognitive habits necessary to evaluate new materials and make sense of them, the following metacognitive strategies may help.

- Connecting New Material to Prior Knowledge: Explicitly show students how new information connects to what they have previously learnt. This practice will help students see the bigger picture and understand the relevance of new content.
- Encourage Active Reflection: Prompt students to reflect on their learning process, such as by asking them to consider how new information fits with their existing knowledge and what strategies they have applied to understand it.
- Facilitate Critical Thinking: Encourage students to analyse new material, helping them to identify key information and its significance for listening comprehension.
- Model Metacognitive Strategies: Demonstrate how to use metacognitive strategies in listening tasks, such as when predicting content, monitoring comprehension, and evaluating understanding.
- Provide Scaffolding: Offer support while students practice metacognitive strategies, gradually reducing assistance as they become more proficient.

However, implementing metacognitive strategies in writing presents several critical challenges. A primary issue is the lack of awareness and training among educators and students, which can lead to a superficial application of these strategies without a deep understanding of their purpose. Integrating metacognitive strategies into an already packed curriculum is another hurdle, often resulting in these strategies being sidelined. Student engagement is crucial but can be difficult to achieve, as some students may resist introspection or fail to see the immediate benefits. Additionally, traditional assessment methods may not effectively capture improvements in metacognitive skills, complicating the feedback process. The diverse needs of learners further complicate implementation, as a one-size-fits-all approach is rarely effective. Time constraints in educational settings also pose a barrier, as developing metacognitive skills requires practice, reflection, and feedback. Finally, resource limitations, such as insufficient training materials and professional development opportunities, can lead to inconsistent application across classrooms.

5.3 Summary

Listening comprehension transcends the simplistic notion of auditory reception, representing a dynamic process of meaning construction that is pivotal in language learning. It holds particular significance for EFL learners, who frequently face unique challenges when cultivating this skill. Despite its recognised importance, the awareness and application of metacognitive listening comprehension strategies are sorely lacking in listening instruction.

Metacognitive strategies encompass deliberate cognitive processes (e.g., monitoring and regulating one's cognitive activities) to enhance listening comprehension. However, teacher metacognition plays a crucial role in realising the full extent of metacognitive facilitation for listening: teachers must first develop their own metacognitive awareness to effectively guide students in employing these strategies.

6 Metacognition in Vocabulary Learning

Studies on vocabulary learning strategies have proceeded for almost thirty years. Numerous theoretical and empirical studies have been conducted, establishing vocabulary learning strategy research firmly within the field of applied linguistics following early work by Gu and Johnson (1996). Despite these advancements, Gu (2018) noted that academic interest in vocabulary learning strategies still requires development. This somewhat ambivalent status stems in part from a series of critiques regarding the definitional fuzziness and lack of rigor when measuring vocabulary learning strategies from the self-regulation perspective (Tseng et al., 2006).

These criticisms have spurred theoretical progress, leading vocabulary learning to be redefined through the lens of metacognition (F. Teng & Mizumoto, 2024). One significant attempt to address these issues is the incorporation of metacognitive strategies into vocabulary learning, a concept rooted in educational psychology (Schraw, 1998). Progress has highlighted the pertinence of a metacognitive perspective in vocabulary learning strategy research, offering a more comprehensive framework to help learners acquire vocabulary.

6.1 Understanding Metacognition in Vocabulary Learning

A wide range of knowledge aspects accompany knowing a word, with each aspect involving varying degrees of strength, detail, and fluency. In a vocabulary instruction course, the curriculum's focus and balance are essential to ensuring the development of well-rounded, usable vocabulary knowledge. According to Nation (2020), the two major conditions for effective vocabulary instruction are the number of encounters with words and the quality of attention given to those words. Vocabulary learning basically hinges on how often words are encountered and the depth of mental processing during each encounter.

Noticing is the most superficial level of attention but remains useful. The next level, retrieval, builds on prior noticing. Receptive retrieval occurs when a learner sees or hears a word and must recall its meaning, often facilitated by extensive reading. Productive retrieval happens when a learner wants to express a meaning and must call to mind the appropriate spoken or written word form. Both receptive and productive retrieval are more influential for learning when they build on previous instances of retrieval or noticing. However, learners' metacognitive awareness is crucial for effectively noticing and understanding the different dimensions of vocabulary knowledge. Metacognitive strategies enable learners to plan, monitor, and evaluate their vocabulary learning processes, thereby enhancing their ability to notice and retrieve words. This heightened awareness helps learners develop a more nuanced approach to vocabulary learning, such that they not only recognise and recall words but also understand and use them proficiently.

Before addressing metacognition in vocabulary learning, it is necessary to clarify the concept of SRL and its presence in vocabulary strategy research. The integration of SRL concepts into this line of research can be traced back to Tseng et al. (2006). They devised a tool to measure self-regulatory capacity in vocabulary learning, marking the beginning of a more structured approach to determining how learners manage vocabulary acquisition. The literature has since explored the intricacies of self-regulatory and self-regulated aspects of vocabulary learning. For instance, Mizumoto (2013) investigated how self-regulation shapes vocabulary learning strategies and outcomes, providing insights into the mechanisms through which people control and direct their learning activities. F. Teng et al. (2024) further examined these concepts, highlighting self-regulation as vital for a growth mindset and effective vocabulary acquisition. As learners better grasp their metacognitive processes, they become more adroit at employing strategies that boost their growth mindset. Significantly enhanced vocabulary learning can then follow (F. Teng, 2024b). Researchers have also considered the criterion-related validity of self-regulated vocabulary learning through composite models (Alamer, Teng, & Mizumoto, 2024); constructs of self-regulated vocabulary learning appear positively and moderately associated with L2 vocabulary achievement. This relationship underscores the role of self-regulation in enhancing vocabulary learning outcomes: it suggests that individuals who regulate their learning processes well tend to achieve higher levels of vocabulary proficiency.

Incorporating SRL into vocabulary learning strategy research has generated several developments.

1) Measurement Tools: The creation of tools to assess self-regulatory capacity has enabled researchers to quantify learners' abilities to manage their vocabulary learning.
2) Effects on Learning Strategies: Understanding how self-regulation influences learning strategies has offered valuable insights into the ways learners can optimise their vocabulary learning.
3) Validity and Achievement: The positive correlations between SRL constructs and vocabulary achievement highlight the practical benefits of fostering language learners' self-regulation.

As research on vocabulary learning strategies increasingly focuses on self-regulatory capacity, a crucial element remains underexplored – metacognition, also known as metacognitive awareness. Self-regulatory capacity and metacognitive awareness are interrelated (Wen et al., 2023). Self-regulatory capacity involves one's ability to manage their thoughts, emotions, and actions using various cognitive and metacognitive strategies, along with motivation, to achieve goals. By contrast, metacognitive awareness refers to one's awareness of their cognitive processes, including knowledge of personal learning strategies and how best to apply them. Growing attention is being paid to the role of metacognition in vocabulary learning, which can be conceptualised as learners' awareness and regulation of their cognitive processes (e.g., planning, monitoring, and evaluating their learning activities) to enhance vocabulary acquisition. This heightened interest in metacognitive strategies is intended to help students become more effective and autonomous in their vocabulary learning endeavours.

The goal of documenting the practices of 'good' language learners is to identify strategies that less successful learners can adopt. Rodgers (2018) argued that (a) effective strategy use is generally associated with more successful vocabulary learning, (b) 'good' learners are proactive in their vocabulary learning, and (c) these learners are flexible in their strategy use for acquiring new words. Such assumptions have been confirmed empirically. F. Teng and Zhang (2024) randomly assigned 120 Chinese university EFL students to 1 of 4 task conditions: 1) reading, 2) reading + gap-fill, 3) reading + writing, and 4) reading + writing with the use of a digital dictionary. The Metacognitive Awareness Inventory was administered to assess participants' metacognitive knowledge and regulation. The standardised parameter estimates for metacognitive regulation were significant at the .001 level for both receptive and productive knowledge. Unexpectedly, however, the standardised parameter estimates for metacognitive knowledge were not significant for either receptive or productive knowledge. In line with F. Teng (2023b), awareness of metacognitive regulation may lead to greater engagement with and use of vocabulary learning strategies, thereby fostering better mastery of both receptive and productive vocabulary knowledge.

Several studies have addressed the longitudinal impact of metacognitive knowledge on vocabulary learning. For example, F. Teng (2022c) explored how enhanced acquisition of metacognitive knowledge could serve as a foundation for understanding and using metacognitive strategies to identify, evaluate, and improve vocabulary learning among primary school learners. The study showed that participants' levels of metacognitive knowledge were strongly associated with their vocabulary knowledge over the school year. The more learners understood their mental and cognitive processes, the better their vocabulary acquisition. Two other studies focused on metacognition and vocabulary learning for minority multilingual learners (F. Teng & Zhang, 2022, 2024a). These articles revealed that learners' cognitive achievements (e.g., the ability to explain strategy use based on learning experiences) predicted their vocabulary learning, including morphological awareness. Furthermore, growth in learners' metacognitive knowledge was linked to improvements in vocabulary learning from a longitudinal perspective.

Several authors have considered the topic of training metacognitive strategies for vocabulary learning. For example, Rasekh and Ranjbary (2003) investigated the effects of explicit instruction on metacognitive strategies using a teaching model with five steps: preparation, presentation, practice, evaluation, and expansion. Findings indicated that the explicit instruction and practice received by the experimental group significantly contributed to these participants' improved lexical knowledge. The training involved teaching participants how to plan their vocabulary learning, set goals within a specific timeframe, select the most appropriate vocabulary learning strategies, monitor strategy use, combine multiple strategies, self-test their mastery of new vocabulary items after initial exposure, manage their study time to include vocabulary practice, and evaluate the entire learning process. Similarly, F. Teng and Reynolds (2019) applied individual and group metacognitive prompts to facilitate incidental vocabulary learning from reading. The prompts included self-addressed questions addressing two components: knowledge of metacognition and regulation of metacognition. Collaborative learning with prompts was identified as the most effective condition for vocabulary learning. The metacognitive prompts in a group setting helped participants become familiar with necessary actions such as searching for various information, monitoring and evaluating this process, conducting argumentation, reasoning, and problem solving. This approach enabled students to engage in peer interaction, which motivated them to reason with one another to understand the text while simultaneously grasping the meanings of difficult words.

Given the insights from numerous studies, metacognition in vocabulary learning can be defined as one's awareness and regulation of their cognitive processes to enhance vocabulary learning. This concept involves understanding how to effectively plan, monitor, and evaluate one's learning activities. Metacognitive awareness lets learners notice and retrieve words more efficiently, facilitating deeper mental processing and better retention. By cultivating metacognitive awareness, learners can set specific goals, choose suitable strategies, and assess their progress – all of which promote more autonomous and effective vocabulary learning. This description highlights the importance of bringing metacognitive training into vocabulary instruction. Doing so can prepare individuals to be more self-regulated and successful in their vocabulary learning efforts.

6.2 Critical Issues

6.2.1 Lack of Attention to Metacognitive Strategies for Vocabulary Learning

As is apparent, people can employ a variety of strategies to learn L2 vocabulary. Several scholars have developed taxonomies of available techniques, with O'Malley and Chamot's (1990) and Oxford's (1990) frameworks being the most highly cited. These taxonomies differentiate between cognitive and metacognitive strategies. Cognitive strategies relate to how learners process the target lexical items. From a practical standpoint, cognitive strategies can be seen as 'hands-on' methods, such as using flashcards as a study tool. Metacognitive strategies, on the other hand, are higher-order approaches concerned with the regulation of learning. These strategies are normally associated with reflective practice and can be subcategorised into planning, monitoring, and evaluating learning.

One critical issue in vocabulary instruction is the frequent use of cognitive strategies – often to the neglect of metacognitive options. Many students lack metacognitive strategies to seek out opportunities for practice and to plan their learning, such as deciding when and how frequently to review items in their vocabulary notebooks. That is not to say that metacognitive strategies are inherently more effective than cognitive ones. However, the awareness and application of metacognitive strategies are noticeably absent from vocabulary learning compared with other language-learning domains (e.g., reading and writing). Teachers, especially in EFL settings, tend to rely heavily on grammar translation and exam-oriented methods. Even when cognitive techniques like flashcards are used, students often remain passive in their learning rather than taking active roles.

Metacognition in Language Teaching 61

Students may be active in rote-memorising a large number of words, but this method should not be suggested as a primary means of vocabulary learning. Vocabulary instruction should be part of a well-balanced language course composed of four equal strands: meaning-focused input, meaning-focused output, language-focused learning, and fluency development (Nation, 2007). Teachers and learners both need to build metacognitive awareness in order to strike this balance. Being able to integrate and use cognitive and metacognitive strategies will allow for a more comprehensive, autonomous approach to vocabulary learning.

6.2.2 Use Reflective Questions to Foster Metacognitive Awareness for Vocabulary Learning

Another critical issue in vocabulary learning is the use of reflective questions to foster metacognitive awareness. Promoting metacognition among students is primarily achieved through posing reflective questions (Teng & Reynolds, 2019). Although teachers mostly employ these as a rounding-off activity, the questions can also be used to encourage metacognitive awareness at all three stages of learning: planning, monitoring, and evaluating. For that reason, reflective questions can serve a variety of purposes in the classroom, enhancing the overall learning experience. These types of questions encourage reflection about the learning of vocabulary items so students start to think deeply about this process.

However, it is often unclear which methods learners apply to reach goals. Reflective questions can be easily incorporated into classroom activities – even in core course components. For instance, these questions could be featured as prompts in a reflective journal or as short-answer questions on tests or assignments. Additionally, when demonstrating metacognitive strategies, teachers could respond to these questions as part of a think-aloud task to model metacognitive practices for students. Unfortunately, many teachers are unaware of how to apply reflective questions at each point of the learning process. Such questions tend to appear intermittently (i.e., within individual lessons) instead of as part of an all-encompassing evaluation strategy. This somewhat fragmented implementation means that students seldom develop a complete understanding of how to plan, monitor, and assess their vocabulary learning through reflective questions.

To address this issue, teachers need to consistently infuse reflective questions into the learning process, such as by making them a regular part of vocabulary instruction. This integration will help students engage more thoroughly with learning strategies, leading to greater metacognitive awareness and more effective vocabulary acquisition. By encouraging regular reflection, students can become more autonomous learners; they will therefore be better prepared to manage their vocabulary learning in a structured, self-regulated manner.

6.3 Summary

This section synthesises ideas from studies related to metacognition in vocabulary learning. The concept refers to learners' awareness and regulation of their cognitive processes to enhance vocabulary acquisition. Metacognitive strategies equip learners with skills to notice and retrieve words more efficiently, facilitating deeper mental processing and better retention. Learners who have honed their metacognitive awareness can set specific goals, choose appropriate strategies, and monitor their progress to acquire vocabulary more independently and fluidly.

This section also underscores the need for metacognitive training in vocabulary learning. It highlights how reflective questions can be used to promote metacognitive awareness at all stages of learning. These questions can be incorporated into various classroom activities (e.g., reflective journals, short-answer questions on tests, and think-aloud tasks). However, the section also points out that many teachers lack awareness of how to incorporate these questions throughout the learning process rather than only in standalone lessons. This disjointed application hinders students from fully developing the skills to plan, monitor, and evaluate their vocabulary learning through reflection. Students can become more autonomous vocabulary learners by making reflection a habit.

7 Assessing Metacognition

Researchers have employed various methods to measure learners' metacognitive awareness, including self-report questionnaires, observations, think-aloud protocols, and interviews (Winne & Perry, 2005). For instance, metacognition can be examined through stimulated recalls and by retrospectively asking learners about their thoughts during task performance (Bui & Kong, 2019). In a review of 123 studies on metacognition assessment, Dinsmore, Alexander, and Loughlin (2008) identified self-report questionnaires as particularly popular due to their cost-effectiveness, suitability for large-scale studies, and ease of administration and scoring. Despite concerns about the reliability of self-report data, these tools have received significant academic attention. Given the variety and popularity of these assessment methods, there is a clear need for a dedicated section on assessing metacognition. Such a section would provide a comprehensive overview of the different assessment tools, elucidate their applications, and evaluate their effectiveness in understanding learners' metacognitive processes, thereby guiding educators and researchers in selecting appropriate methods for their specific contexts.

7.1 Understanding Assessment Tools for Metacognition

The following sub-sections introduce select tools for testing metacognition in different domains.

7.1.1 Metacognition Scale in Educational Psychology

Metacognitive Awareness Inventory (MAI)

The Metacognitive Awareness Inventory (MAI), which Schraw and Dennison (1994) developed, is a popular scale for measuring metacognitive awareness in adolescents and adults. This survey consists of fifty-two items divided into eight factors that constitute two dimensions: knowledge of cognition (seventeen items) and regulation of cognition (thirty-five items). The knowledge dimension covers declarative, procedural, and conditional knowledge; the regulation dimension includes planning, information management strategies, monitoring, debugging strategies, and evaluation. The MAI is a reliable tool for initially assessing metacognitive awareness. It is also effective for evaluating lower-performing students who often exhibit deficiencies in comprehension monitoring.

7.1.2 Language-Learning Strategies

The Strategy Inventory of Language Learning (SILL)

The Strategy Inventory for Language Learning (SILL), created by Oxford (1990), is a fifty-item instrument designed to test language learners' use of various strategies (i.e., in the memory, cognitive, metacognitive, compensation, affective, and social domains). SILL arose from the observation that successful language learners tend to deploy useful strategies more frequently than less successful learners and that awareness of these strategies can help predict language-learning performance. Teachers using SILL can gain a comprehensive strategy profile of their students and determine the types of strategies learners adopt when studying English as a second or foreign language.

7.1.3 Metacognition Scale for Listening

Metacognitive Awareness Listening Questionnaire (MALQ)

Vandergrift et al. (2006) constructed the Metacognitive Awareness Listening Questionnaire (MALQ) to assess L2 listeners' metacognitive awareness and perceived use of strategies while listening to oral texts. The MALQ contains twenty-one items across five factors: problem solving, planning and evaluation, mental translation, person knowledge, and directed attention. It was established based on Flavell's (1979) model of metacognitive knowledge (i.e., person, task, and strategy knowledge). Students can use the MALQ to identify their current level of metacognitive awareness and to chart their strategy use and listening comprehension awareness over time. The MALQ may also be used for metacognitive training to help learners become skilled listeners who self-regulate their metacognitive comprehension automatically. In addition, teachers can use the MALQ as a diagnostic or consciousness-raising tool to understand students' metacognitive awareness in listening comprehension.

Mobile-Assisted Self-Regulated Listening Strategy Questionnaire (MSRLS-Q)

Zhou et al. (2024) developed the Mobile-Assisted Self-Regulated Listening Strategy Questionnaire (MSRLS-Q) to account for mobile technologies' transformative effects on L2 listening. The tool is based on a 31-item, five-factor model of students' pre-, during-, and post-listening strategies: goal setting and mobile resource planning, cognitive and metacognitive multimedia listening, mobile-assisted motivational control, structuring online social space, and listening evaluation and adaptation. These areas align with Zimmerman's (2001) framework, which describes SRL as a holistic, cyclical process comprising forethought, performance, and self-reflection. This self-regulated listening process includes task-specific strategies during listening, setting listening goals, planning and seeking resources, and evaluating and adapting listening practices – all key components of SRL.

7.1.4 Metacognition scale for reading

Metacognitive Awareness of Reading Strategies Inventory (MARSI)

Mokhtari and Reichard (2002) created the Metacognitive Awareness of Reading Strategies Inventory (MARSI) to assess 6th- through 12th-grade students' metacognitive awareness and perceived use of reading strategies while reading academic or school-related materials. MARSI includes three factors. The first, Global Reading Strategies, contains 13 items focused on reading strategies to globally analyse the text. The second factor is Problem-Solving Strategies, composed of eight items related to strategies for solving problems when text becomes difficult to read. The third factor is Support Reading Strategies; it contains nine items measuring the use of outside reference materials, note taking, and other support strategies. MARSI provides feedback for assessing the degree to which a student is or is not aware of the cognitive processes for reading. The results can provide information for learners to increase their awareness of their own comprehension processes and help teachers to understand students' strategy use in reading.

7.1.5 Metacognition scale for writing

Writing Strategies for Self-Regulated Learning Questionnaire (WSSRLQ)

The Writing Strategies for Self-Regulated Learning Questionnaire (WSSRLQ), which L. Teng and Zhang (2016) developed, is one of the most-cited scales in writing. It includes forty items and nine factors: goal-oriented monitoring and evaluating, idea planning, peer learning, feedback handling, interest enhancement, emotional control, motivational self-talk, text processing, and course memory. The WSSRLQ can be used as a self-evaluation tool for students to appraise their degree of awareness of writing strategies to reflect on their writing strategy use when developing writing skills in EFL contexts. The instrument provides insights into self-regulated writing strategies from cognitive, metacognitive, social-behavioural, and motivational regulation perspectives.

Metacognitive Academic Writing Strategies Questionnaire (MAWSQ)

F. Teng et al. (2022) constructed the MAWSQ through a five-step procedure: item generation, reference consultation, initial piloting, psychometric evaluation, and exploratory factor analysis (EFA). The MAWSQ has two main components, metacognitive knowledge and metacognitive regulation. The authors established three categories of metacognitive knowledge (i.e., declarative knowledge, procedural knowledge, and conditional knowledge). Five categories (i.e., planning, monitoring, evaluating, debugging, and information management) were specified for metacognitive regulation. Confirmatory factor analysis (CFA) revealed an eight-factor correlated model of metacognitive strategies for EFL academic writing with standardised regression weights as well as a one-factor second-order model of metacognitive strategies for EFL academic writing. The findings also supported the roles of different MAWSQ subcategories in predicting EFL learners' academic writing performance.

Self-Regulatory Writing Strategy Questionnaire (SRWSQ) for Young Learners

F. Teng et al. (2022) assessed the Self-Regulatory Writing Strategy Questionnaire (SRWSQ) for young EFL learners. The study featured a factorial design; EFA and CFA were performed to validate the inferences and uses of the questionnaire. The CFA results confirmed six factors for the thirty-item instrument: writing planning, goal-oriented monitoring, goal-oriented evaluation, emotional control, memorisation strategies, and metacognitive judgement.

Metacognition-Based Student Feedback Literacy (MSFL)

F. Teng and Ma's (2024) study may be the first to evaluate metacognition-based feedback literacy. The findings validated their tool's factorial structure, with *knowing*, *being*, and *doing* representing three components of metacognition-based student feedback literacy. These three factors shed new light on our understanding of metacognitive awareness and skills in student feedback literacy. For the knowing dimension, feedback literate writers need to possess knowledge of writing tasks, knowledge of academic writing, knowledge of learning through assessment, and strategy knowledge. For the being dimension, findings supported the roles of self-perceived motivation and confidence in adjusting one's emotions in response to feedback. For the doing dimension, the results showed that student writers need to deploy both feedback-related writing strategies (i.e., feedback-related planning, monitoring, and evaluation strategies) and feedback-related strategies in participation (i.e., various strategies employed when seeking, generating, processing, or using feedback).

Metacognitive Writing Strategies for Self-Regulated Learning (MWSSRL) in Multimedia Writing Contexts

F. Teng and Qin (2024) validated the Metacognitive Writing Strategies for Self-Regulated Learning (MWSSRL) instrument, which comprises fifty-two items. A CFA substantiated the instrument's factorial structure, including emotional control, motivation and interests, debugging strategies, declarative knowledge, procedural knowledge, information management strategies, corrective feedback, planning, monitoring, and evaluating. The MWSSRL demonstrated satisfactory psychometric properties for assessing metacognitive writing strategies in SRL. Findings confirmed this tool's validity for measuring the multifaceted structure of metacognitive writing strategies that learners use in an EFL multimedia writing context. The proposed eleven metacognitive writing strategies were significantly correlated yet conceptually and empirically distinct. All metacognitive writing strategies were validated via CFA and conceptually interpreted with reference to the four core components of SRL: motivational regulation, metacognitive knowledge, social behaviour, and metacognitive regulation.

Self-Regulation Scale for Multimedia Writing (SRSMW)

F. Teng and Zhang (2024) validated the Self-Regulated Scale for Multimedia Writing (SRSMW) through a three-step process of consulting relevant theories and literature, cross-checking with interviews, and performing EFA. Their analysis uncovered five key factors (goal setting, strategic planning, elaboration, self-evaluation, and help-seeking) clustered under the umbrella of self-regulation. The first factor, goal setting, comprises five writing strategies that span different phases of self-regulation: forethought (setting a goal for multimedia writing [Item 2]); performance control (employing goal-directed actions [Items 4 and 5] and monitoring performance [Item 1]); and self-reflection on using various multimedia tools (Item 3). The second factor, strategic planning, consists of five validated strategies: course preparation (Item 6), evaluation of multimedia platforms (Item 7), planning and evaluating strategies (Item 8), time management (Item 9), and online resource planning (Item 10). The third factor, elaboration, focuses on connecting new information to prior knowledge (Items 13 and 14), using online information (Items 11 and 12), and providing detailed explanations of social phenomena (Item 15). The fourth factor, self-evaluation, involves learners' self-assessment of language use (Item 19), course evaluation (Items 18 and 20), content evaluation (Item 16), and multimedia tool evaluation (Item 17). The fifth factor is help-seeking; it describes strategies that require learners to collaborate with others to enhance writing performance, primarily focusing on seeking assistance from teachers and peers (Items 21–25).

7.1.6 Metacognition Scale for Vocabulary Learning

Self-Regulating Capacity in Vocabulary Learning Scale (SRCvoc)

Tseng et al. (2006) reported that the overall (i.e., composite) reliability of the Self-Regulating Capacity in Vocabulary Learning (SRCvoc) scale was impressively high at 0.92. They demonstrated that the latent construct of SRCvoc can be effectively represented and measured through five indicators: commitment control, metacognitive control, satiation control, emotion control, and environmental control. Consequently, they argued that the SRCvoc is a meaningful and valid measure, providing a foundation for exploring the theoretical nature of self-regulation. Their findings highlight the definitional ambiguity surrounding language-learning strategies and the inadequacy of existing psychometric instruments designed to measure strategic learning capacity. To address these issues, the researchers operationalised strategic learning and introduced the SRCvoc to measure language learners' self-regulation in a context-specific manner. Further discussions on the SRCvoc can be found in studies published in the same journal, *Applied Linguistics*, by Alamer et al. (2024) and Mizumoto and Takeuchi (2012); their articles delve into this scale's application and implications in the field of vocabulary learning.

Metacognitive Knowledge of Vocabulary Learning Questionnaire (MKVLQ)

F. Teng and Mizumoto (2024) developed and validated a scale for assessing metacognitive knowledge in vocabulary learning. The scale is structured around three sub-dimensions – person, task, and strategies – identified through EFA and CFA. These factors align with Flavell's (1979) framework of metacognitive knowledge. The sub-dimension of metacognitive knowledge of the self (person) includes six items, focusing on understanding new words essential for text comprehension, memorising the spelling and meanings of new words, seeking reading material that suits personal interests, understanding logical development, looking for explanations in the text or a dictionary, and maintaining engagement in reading despite encountering unknown words. The sub-dimension of metacognitive knowledge of the task also contains six items: topics included the use of contextual encoding; finding interest in learning word structures (e.g., prefixes, suffixes); making up sentences using new words; applying newly learnt words in real-life situations; using newly learnt words in imaginary scenarios; and taking notes while reading. The sub-dimension of metacognitive knowledge of the strategies comprises four items, centred on understanding the meaning as intended by the author, planning what needs to be done and in what sequence, monitoring comprehension, and reflecting on how the word relates to broader concepts. This scale is a robust tool for evaluating metacognitive knowledge in vocabulary learning and offers valuable insights into learners' cognitive processes and strategies.

7.1.7 Metacognitive Knowledge (MCK) Test for Young Learners' Foreign Language Learning

F. Teng and Zhang (2024) validated a metacognitive knowledge (MCK) test for young learners' foreign language learning. This test comprises thirty tasks, each designed with three distinct scenarios, resulting in a holistic assessment that covers a range of metacognitive strategies relevant to foreign language learning. To help young learners better understand the tasks and verbalise their metacognitive strategies, three black-and-white drawings are presented to illustrate the situations. EFA was employed to distil the essence of metacognitive knowledge, suggesting that memory, learning, and comprehension strategies are interconnected through higher-order metacognitive understanding. CFA provided statistical confirmation of the model's fit, indicating that a single overarching factor

Metacognition in Language Teaching 69

of metacognitive knowledge accounts for the correlations observed among memory (8 items), learning (4 items), and comprehension strategies (12 items).

7.2 Critical Issues

7.2.1 Doubts about Overrelying on Learners' Self-Report Data

Assessing metacognitive awareness presents significant challenges, particularly in the realm of testing. One critical issue is an overreliance on learners' self-report data. Self-report questionnaires, while convenient and easy to administer, often fail to capture the extent of learners' internal cognitive and emotional processes. Learners may struggle to articulate their thoughts and feelings, leading to incomplete or biased responses. Additionally, learners' language proficiency can influence their answers, potentially skewing results and not reflecting respondents' genuine metacognitive awareness.

Despite these limitations, self-report questionnaires remain popular due to their practicality. Alternative methods, such as think-aloud protocols (i.e., where learners verbalise their thought processes while engaging in a task), can provide more detailed data. However, these procedures are usually challenging to administer; they require considerable time and resources. Researchers instead tend to favour more straightforward approaches such as surveys, using conventional statistical techniques like EFA and CFA for validation purposes.

Several strategies can be employed to enhance the validity of surveys assessing metacognitive awareness. First, mixed-method approaches can provide a more comprehensive understanding. For example, combining self-report questionnaires with qualitative methods such as interviews or think-aloud protocols can help triangulate data and offer deeper insights into learners' metacognitive processes. Second, ensuring questionnaire items' clarity and relevance is crucial. Items should be designed to be understood by learners of varying proficiency levels and should target specific aspects of metacognitive awareness. Piloting a questionnaire with a small group of learners and refining items based on respondents' feedback can help improve the instrument's reliability and validity. Third, adopting technology to facilitate data collection can also enhance validity. For instance, using digital tools that allow learners to record their thoughts in real time during language tasks can provide more precise, immediate reflections of metacognitive strategies. Finally, ongoing training for researchers and educators in administering and interpreting these assessments is essential. Ensuring that those involved in the research process are well-versed in the nuances of metacognitive assessment can mitigate biases and improve overall data quality.

7.2.2 Lack of Attention to Assessing Young Learners' Metacognitive Awareness

Another critical issue in the assessment of metacognitive awareness is the disproportionate focus on university students or adults to the relative neglect of young learners. While evaluating young learners' metacognitive awareness presents unique challenges, it is nonetheless important – and, in fact, urgently necessary. A key reason for this imbalance is the difficulty in creating and administering assessments suitable for young learners. Children may have limited abilities to reflect on and describe their cognitive processes, reducing the effectiveness of traditional self-report questionnaires. However, this issue should not deter researchers from pursuing this line of enquiry. It in fact highlights the need to devise age-appropriate methods for evaluating young learners' metacognitive awareness.

Longitudinal studies by F. Teng and Zhang (2021, 2022, 2024a) have demonstrated that young learners' initial levels of metacognitive knowledge are significantly related to later development in this area. These findings suggest that early metacognitive awareness can have lasting impacts on learners' cognitive and academic growth. Therefore, researchers must pay more attention to early stages of metacognitive development.

7.3 Summary

This section synthesises key assessment tools for understanding learners' metacognitive awareness across various domains, including listening, reading, writing, and vocabulary learning. By addressing associated obstacles and employing a combination of strategies, researchers can enhance assessment tools' accuracy and reliability. Data will then offer a firmer sense of respondents' cognitive processes and improve language-learning outcomes.

The section also discusses the need to measure young learners' metacognitive awareness. By expanding the focus to include this demographic, researchers can gain valuable information about the developmental trajectory of metacognitive awareness. Such insights can inform educational practices and policies aimed at nurturing metacognitive skills from an early age, thereby supporting lifelong learning and cognitive development.

8 Conclusion on Metacognition in Language Teaching

Metacognitive instruction can be highly effective for enhancing listening, reading, writing, and vocabulary learning. Teaching metacognitive skills provides instructors with strategies to reshape their classroom environment, enhance students' capabilities in learning and using strategies, and improve students' cognitive abilities and motivation for language learning.

Certain principles are crucial when considering pedagogy for metacognitive instruction: activating learners' prior knowledge; encouraging reflections on what they know and what they want to learn; and fostering active engagement in setting goals, monitoring, and evaluating one's learning process and outcomes. Anderson's (2002) five components for understanding students' roles in metacognitive instruction are particularly useful.

1) Preparing and Planning for Learning: Helping students set clear, achievable goals.
2) Building Conscious Decisions in Selecting and Using Learning Strategies: Encouraging students to make informed choices about their learning strategies.
3) Monitoring and Keeping Track of Strategy Use: Teaching students to continually assess their strategies' effectiveness.
4) Orchestrating and Coordinating Various Strategies for Learning: Guiding students in combining strategies effectively.
5) Building Awareness of Strategy Use: Enhancing students' awareness of how and why they use certain strategies.

Teachers should focus on different components of metacognitive knowledge (person, task, and strategy) and target aspects of writing that enhance learners' metacognition.

In reflection on teachers' roles in metacognitive instruction, effective metacognitive instruction also requires teachers to be aware of their roles, including reflecting on their own pedagogy, knowledge, and practices. Teachers are key players in explaining and modelling learner strategies, often in unpredictable settings. Working with students who have diverse abilities and levels of motivation calls for a reflective approach to evaluating individual differences in the learning process. If metacognitive instruction focuses on students' awareness in planning, implementing, monitoring, and evaluating their learning, then teachers must also develop awareness to plan, implement, monitor, and evaluate their teaching (Svalberg, 2007). Hiver and Whitehead (2018) offered several suggestions regarding teachers' roles in metacognitive instruction.

1) Being Proficient in Their Own Language(s): Teachers should serve as language models for their students.
2) Building Metalinguistic Knowledge: Teachers should understand their linguistic choices and these choices' impacts on students.

3) Promoting Intercultural Competence: Teachers should encourage students to monitor and adjust their thinking and interactions with others.
4) Understanding Language-Learning Processes: Teachers should help students take control of their learning by assigning them active roles.

Despite the benefits of metacognitive instruction, teachers face challenges in implementing it. They may lack the knowledge or training to enhance learners' metacognitive awareness or doubt the effectiveness of curriculum changes. Without sufficient autonomy to develop materials for metacognitive instruction, teachers might even be reluctant to adopt this approach. Productive mentorship can support teachers in infusing greater metacognitive thought and action into their practice. These types of partnerships can build a network for critical reflection and adaptability.

Teachers should also consider learners' emotions and cognition in complex learning environments. Being aware of students' affective responses, such as enjoyment or anxiety, can help encourage learners to control their metacognitive knowledge and interest in tasks.

It is also crucial to examine L2 learners' metacognition in relation to their behavioural patterns, such as motivation. Learners may lack the drive to assume an active role in their learning. Engaging students in activities that help them understand their language-learning skills and that provide opportunities to activate prior knowledge can foster introspection on old and new knowledge. Teachers and students can collaborate to reflect on the language-learning process, transferring metacognitive strategies to new contexts.

Educators must consider students' language proficiency levels, which can influence the effectiveness of metacognitive instruction for reading comprehension (Zhang et al., 2008) and writing (Ma & F. Teng, 2021). Sparks and Ganschow (1993) argued that L1 achievement affects L2 aptitude and proficiency. Linking inefficient use of language-learning strategies with poor foreign language outcomes can be problematic because learners with low L1 achievement may struggle to become metacognitively aware and to use necessary strategies (Sparks & Ganschow, 1993). Thus, higher-proficiency learners are more likely to employ effective reading and writing strategies, whereas lower-proficiency learners may rely excessively on bottom-up decoding and spelling.

Teachers also need to make metacognitive instruction explicit for low-proficiency learners. Difficulties in L2 learning often stem from challenges in L1 skills and processing L2 phonological, orthographic, syntactic, and semantic relationships. Combining metacognitive strategies with linguistic and schematic knowledge can help learners reconstruct clues, interpret meaning, summarise information, and make inferences when reading and writing. Explicit instruction can enable learners to use different strategies to coherently understand text or writing assignments. In conclusion, while metacognitive instruction has a long way to go, it shows great promise for enhancing language learning. By addressing associated challenges and focusing on explicit instruction, particularly for low-proficiency learners, teachers can help students develop robust metacognitive skills that support lifelong learning and cognitive development.

As we anticipate the future of metacognitive awareness in language learning, AI technologies like ChatGPT are poised to play a pivotal role. Mizumoto (2023) introduced the Metacognitive Resource Use (MRU) framework, which integrates data-driven learning within a broad ecosystem of generative AI tools. This framework emphasises metacognitive knowledge and regulation, capitalising on the strengths of both data-driven learning (DDL) and generative AI (GenAI) while addressing their limitations. The importance of metacognitive awareness in effectively utilising AI resources is underscored. Abdelhalim (2024) explored learners' metacognitive awareness in using ChatGPT to enhance research skills, collecting both quantitative and qualitative data from twenty-seven EFL undergraduate students over one semester. The study revealed distinct differences in ChatGPT usage between students with low and high metacognitive awareness, with a positive correlation between metacognitive awareness scores and students' perceptions of ChatGPT. F. Teng (2024c) examined how different levels of metacognitive awareness influenced students' experiences and perceptions. Using a mixed-method research design, data from forty EFL undergraduates in a semester-long writing course revealed significant differences in writing motivation, engagement, self-efficacy, and collaborative writing tendencies. A positive correlation was also found between metacognitive awareness scores and students' perceptions and practices of using ChatGPT. Interview data highlighted a spectrum of behaviours, from simply copying text to effectively using ChatGPT for writing feedback, among students with varying levels of metacognitive awareness.

Exploring metacognitive awareness in the context of using ChatGPT presents promising opportunities for enhancing our understanding of how individuals regulate and manage their cognitive processes. This exploration is particularly relevant as learners increasingly engage with AI tools like ChatGPT to support their writing endeavours. As we move forward, it is likely that the role of metacognitive awareness in the effective utilisation of ChatGPT will become a significant trend, especially in EFL settings. Understanding how learners' metacognitive skills influence their interaction with ChatGPT can provide valuable insights into optimising educational practices and improving learning outcomes. By focusing on the nuances of metacognitive awareness, educators can better support students in harnessing the full potential of AI technologies for language learning and beyond.

References

Abdelhalim, S. M. (2024). Using ChatGPT to promote research competency: English as a Foreign Language undergraduates' perceptions and practices across varied metacognitive awareness levels. *Journal of Computer Assisted Learning*. https://doi.org/10.1111/jcal.12948.

Alamer, A., Teng, M. F., & Mizumoto, A. (2024). Revisiting the construct validity of Self-regulating capacity in vocabulary learning scale: The confirmatory composite analysis (CCA) approach. *Applied Linguistics, amae023*. https://doi.org/10.1093/applin/amae023.

Anderson, N. J. (2002). *The role of metacognition in second language teaching and learning*. Washington, DC: Center for Applied Linguistics, ERIC. Clearinghouse on Languages and Linguistics.

Anderson, N. J. (2008). Metacognition and good language learners. In C. Griffiths (ed.), *Lessons from good language learners* (pp. 99–110). Cambridge: Cambridge University Press.

Azevedo, R. (2020). Reflections on the field of metacognition: Issues, challenges, and opportunities. *Metacognition and Learning*, *15*, 91–98.

Baddeley, A. (2003). Working memory: Looking back and looking forward. *Nature Reviews Neuroscience*, *4*(10), 829–839.

Baker, L. (2015). Developmental differences in metacognition: Implications for metacognitively oriented reading instruction. In S. E. Israel, C. C. Block, K. L. Bauserman, & K. Kinnucan-Welsch (eds.), *Metacognition in literacy learning: Theory, assessment, instruction, and professional development* (pp. 61–79). New York: Routledge.

Baker, L. (2017). The development of metacognitive knowledge and control of comprehension: Contributors and consequences. In K. Mokhtari (ed.), *Improving reading comprehension through metacognitive reading instruction* (pp. 1–31). Lanham, MD: Roman and Littlefield.

Bereiter, C., & Scardamalia, M. (1987). *The psychology of written composition*. New York: Routledge.

Boekaerts, M. (1997). Self-regulated learning: A new concept embraced by researchers, policy makers, educators, teachers, and students. *Learning and Instruction*, *7*(2), 161–186.

Brinck, I., & Liljenfors, R. (2013). The developmental origin of metacognition. *Infant and Child Development*, *22*(1), 85–101. https://doi.org/10.1002/icd.1749.

Brown, A. L. (1987). Metacognition, executive control, self-regulation, and other more mysterious mechanisms. In F. E. Weinert & R. H. Kluwe (eds.),

Metacognition, motivation, and understanding (pp. 65–116). Hillsdale, New Jersey: Lawrence Erlbaum Associates.

Bui, G., & Kong, A. (2019). Metacognitive instruction for peer review interaction in L2 writing. *Journal of Writing Research, 11*(2), 357–392.

Dimmitt, C., & McCormick, C. B. (2012). Metacognition in education. In K. R. Harris, S. Graham, & T. Urdan (Eds.), *APA educational psychology handbook, Vol 1: Theories, constructs, and critical issues* (pp. 157–187). Washington, DC: American Psychological Association.

Dinsmore, D. L., Alexander, P. A., & Loughlin, S. M. (2008). Focusing the conceptual lens on metacognition, self-regulation, and self-regulated learning. *Educational Psychology Review, 20*, 391–409.

Efklides, A. (2001). The systemic nature of metacognitive experiences. In P. Chambers, M. Izaute, & P.-J. Marescaux (eds.), *Metacognition: Process, function and use* (pp. 19–34). Dordrecht, Netherlands: Kluwer.

Efklides, A. (2006). Metacognition and affect: What can metacognitive experiences tell us about the learning process? *Educational Research Review, 1*, 3–14.

Efklides, A. (2008). Metacognition: Defining its facets and levels of functioning in relation to self-regulation and co-regulation. *European Psychologist, 13*, 277–287.

Fairbanks, C. M., Duffy, G. G., Faircloth, B. S. et al. (2010). Beyond knowledge: Exploring why some teachers are more thoughtfully adaptive than others. *Journal of Teacher Education, 61* (1–2), 161–171.

Flavell, J. H. (1976). Metacognitive aspects of problem solving. In L. B. Resnick (ed.), *The nature of intelligence* (pp. 231–235). Hillsdale, NJ: Lawrence Erlbaum Associates.

Flavell, J. H. (1979). Metacognition and cognitive monitoring: A new era of cognitive developmental inquiry. *American Psychologist, 34*, 906–911.

Flavell, J. H. (1985). *Cognitive development* (2nd ed.). Englewood Cliffs, NJ: Prentice-Hall.

Flavell, J. H. (1987). Speculations about the nature and development of metacognition. In F. E. Weinert and R. H. Kluwe (eds.), *Metacognition, Motivation and Understanding* (pp. 21–29). Hillsdale, NJ: Erlbaum.

Fleming, S. M., Dolan, R. J., & Frith, C. D. (2012). Metacognition: Computation, biology and function. *Philosophical transactions of the Royal Society of London. Series B, Biological sciences, 367*(1594), 1280–1286. https://doi.org/10.1098/rstb.2012.0021

Flower, L., & Hayes, J. R. (1981). A cognitive process theory of writing. *Composition and Communication, 32*(4), 365–387.

Gass, S. M., & Selinker, L. (2008). *Second language acquisition: An introductory course* (5th ed). New York: Routledge.

Goh, C. (2000). A cognitive perspective on language learners' listening comprehension problems. *System, 28,* 55–75. https://doi.org/10.1016/S0346-251X(99)00060-3

Goh, C. (2008). Metacognitive instruction for second language listening development: Theory, practice and research implications. *RELC Journal, 39*(2), 188–213.

Goh, C. (2018). Metacognition in second language listening. In J. Liontas (ed.), *The TESOL encyclopedia of English language teaching* (pp. 1–7). Hoboken, NJ: John Wiley & Sons.

Goh, C. (2023). Learners' cognitive processing problems during comprehension as a basis for L2 listening research. *System, 119,* 103164.

Goh, C., & Taib, Y. (2006). Metacognitive instruction in listening for young learners. *ELT Journal, 60*(3), 222–232.

Goh, C., & Vandergrift, L. (2021). *Teaching and learning second language listening: Metacognition in action.* New York: Routledge.

Graham, S. (2006). Listening comprehension: The learners' perspective. *System, 34*(2), 165–182.

Graham, S., Harris, K. R., MacArthur, C., & Santangelo, T. (2018). Self-regulation and writing. In D. Schunk & J. Greene (eds.), *Handbook of self-regulation of learning and performance* (2nd ed., pp. 138–152). New York: Routledge.

Gu, P. Y. (2018). Validation of an online questionnaire of vocabulary learning strategies for ESL learners. *Studies in Second Language Learning and Teaching, 8*(2), 325–350.

Gu, Y., & Johnson, R. K. (1996). Vocabulary learning strategies and language learning outcomes. *Language Learning, 46*(4), 643–679.

Hacker, D. J., Keener, M. C., & Kircher, J. C. (2009). Writing is applied metacognition. In D. J. Hacker, J. Dunlosky, & A. C. Graesser (eds.), *Handbook of metacognition in education* (pp. 154–172). New York: Routledge.

Harris, K. R., Graham, S., Brindle, M., & Sandmel, K. (2009). Metacognition and children's writing. In D. J. Hacker, J. Dunlosky, and A. C. Graesser (eds.), *Handbook of metacognition in education* (pp. 131–153). New York: Routledge.

Hayes, J. (1996). A new framework for understanding cognition and affect in writing. In M. Levy & S. Ransdell (eds.), *The science of writing: Theories, methods, individual differences, and applications* (pp. 1–27). Mahwah, NJ: Erlbaum.

Haukås, Å. (2018). Metacognition in language learning and teaching: An overview. In Å. Haukås, C. Bjørke, & M. Dypedahl (eds.), *Metacognition in language learning and teaching* (pp. 11–20). Routledge.

Haukås, Å., Bjørke, C., & Dypedahl, M. (2018). (eds.). *Metacognition in language learning and teaching*. New York: Routledge.

Hertzog, C. (2016). Aging and metacognitive control. In J. Dunlosky & S. K. Tauber (eds.), *Oxford library of psychology: The Oxford handbook of metamemory* (pp. 537–558). New York: Oxford University Press.

Hiver, P., & Whitehead, E. K. (2018). Teaching metacognitively: Adaptive inside-out thinking in the language classroom. In Å. Haukås, C. Bjørke, & M. Dypedahl (eds.), *Metacognition in Language learning and teaching* (pp. 243–262). New York: Routledge.

Kellogg, R. (1996). A model of working memory. In M. C. Levy & S. Ransdell (eds.), *The science of writing* (pp. 57–72). Mahwah: Lawrence Erlbaum Associates.

Kellogg, R. T. (2008). Training writing skills: A cognitive development perspective. *Journal of Writing Research*, *1*, 1–26. https://doi.org/10.17239/jowr-2008.01.01.1.

Kizilcec, R. F., Pérez-Sanagustín, M., & Maldonado, J. J. (2017). Self-regulated learning strategies predict learner behavior and goal attainment in massive open online courses. *Computers & Education*, *104*, 18–33.

Koriat, A. (2007). Metacognition and consciousness. In P. D. Zelazo, M. Moscovich, & E. Thompson (eds.), *The Cambridge handbook of consciousness* (pp. 289–325). New York: Cambridge University Press.

Kress, G. (1982). *Learning to write*. London: Routledge & Kegan Paul.

Larkin, S. (2009). Socially mediated metacognition and learning to write. *Thinking Skills & Creativity*, *4*(3), 149–159.

Lehtonen, T. (2000). Awareness of strategies is not enough: How learners can give each other confidence to use them. *Language Awareness*, *9*(2), 64–77.

Lockl, K., & Schneider, W. (2006). Precursors of metamemory in young children: The role of theory of mind and metacognitive vocabulary. *Metacognition and Learning*, *1*(1), 15–31.

Ma, J., & Teng, F. (2021). Metacognitive knowledge development of students with differing levels of writing proficiency in a process-oriented course: An action research study. In B. L. Reynolds & F. Teng. (eds.), *Innovative approaches in Teaching writing to Chinese speakers* (pp. 92–117). Berlin: DeGruyter Mouton.

McLeod, B., & McLaughlin, B. (1986). Restructuring or automaticity? Reading in a second language. *Language Learning*, *36*(2), 109–123.

Mizumoto, A. (2013). Effects of self-regulated vocabulary learning process on self-efficacy. *Innovation in Language Learning & Teaching*, *7*(3), 253–265.

Mizumoto, A. (2023). Data-driven learning meets Generative AI: Introducing the framework of metacognitive resource use. *Applied Corpus Linguistics*, *3*(3), 100074. https://doi.org/10.1016/j.acorp.2023.100074

Mizumoto, A. & Takeuchi. O. (2012). Adaptation and validation of Self-regulating capacity in vocabulary learning scale. *Applied Linguistics*, *33*, 83–91. https://doi.org/10.1093/applin/amr044

Mokhtari, K., & Reichard, C. A. (2002). Assessing students' metacognitive awareness of reading strategies. *Journal of Educational Psychology*, *94*(2), 249–259.

Nation, I. S. P. (2007). The four strands. *Innovation in Language Learning and Teaching*, *1*(1), 1–12.

Nation, I. S. P. (2022). The different aspects of vocabulary knowledge. In S. Webb (ed.), *The Routledge handbook of vocabulary studies* (pp. 15–29). New York: Routledge.

Nguyen, L. T. C., & Gu, Y. Q. (2013). Strategy-based instruction: A learner-focused approach to developing learner autonomy. *Language Teaching Research*, *17*, 9–30.

Norman, E., Pfuhl, G., Saele, R. et al. (2019). Metacognition in psychology. *Review of General Psychology*, *23*, 403–424.

O'Malley, J. M., & Chamot, A. U. (1990). *Learning strategies in second language acquisition*. Cambridge, England: Cambridge University Press.

Oxford, R. (1990). *Language learning strategies: What every teacher should know*. Boston: Heinle & Heinle.

Paris, S., Cross, D. R., & Lipson, M. Y. (1984). Informed strategies for learning: A program to improve children's reading awareness and comprehension. *Journal of Educational Psychology*, *76*, 1239–1252.

Pennequin, V., Sorel, O., & Mainguy, M. (2010). Metacognition, executive functions and aging: The effect of training in the use of metacognitive skills to solve mathematical word problems. *Journal of Adult Development*, *17*(3), 168–176. http://dx.doi.org/10.1007/s10804-010-9098-3

Pressley, M., & Gaskins, I. W. (2006). Metacognitively competent reading comprehension is constructively responsive reading: How can such reading be developed in students? *Metacognition and Learning*, *1*, 99–113.

Rasekh, Z. E., & Ranjbary, R. (2003). Metacognitive strategy training for vocabulary learning. *TESL-EJ*, *7*(2), 1–18.

Rose, H. (2012). Reconceptualizing strategic learning in the face of self-regulation: Throwing language learning strategies out with the bathwater. *Applied Linguistics*, *33*, 92–98.

References

Rost, M. (2016). *Teaching and researching listening* (3rd ed.). New York: Routledge.

Rodgers, J. (2018). Teaching/Developing vocabulary through metacognition. In J. I. Liontas (ed.), *The TESOL encyclopedia of English language teaching* (pp. 1–6). Hoboken, NJ: John Wiley & Sons.

Sato, M. (2022). Metacognition. In S. Li, P. Hiver, & M. Papi (eds.), *The Routledge handbook of second language acquisition and individual differences* (pp. 95–108). New York: Routledge.

Schraw, G. A. (1998). Promoting general metacognitive awareness. *Instructional Science, 26,* 113–125.

Schraw, G. A. (2001). Promoting general metacognitive awareness. In H. J. Hartman (ed.), *Metacognition in learning and instruction: Theory, research and practice* (pp. 3–16). New York: Springer.

Schraw, G., & Dennison, R. S. (1994). Assessing metacognitive awareness. *Contemporary Educational Psychology, 19,* 460–475.

Shen, X., & Teng, M. F. (2024). Three-wave cross-lagged model on the correlations between critical thinking skills, self-directed learning competency and AI-assisted writing. *Thinking Skills & Creativity.* https://doi.org/10.1016/j.tsc.2024.101524.

Sparks, R., & Ganschow, L. (1993). Searching for the cognitive locus of foreign language learning problems: Linking first and second language learning. *Modern Language Journal, 77,* 289–302.

Sweller, J. (1988). Cognitive load during problem solving: Effects on learning. *Cognitive Science, 12*(2), 257–285.

Svalberg, A. M. (2007). Language awareness and language learning. *Language Teaching, 40*(4), 287–308.

Sun, Q., Pan, H., & Zhan, I. (2024). Untangling the relationship between English as a foreign language learners' metacognitive experiences and writing proficiency: A mixed-methods approach. *System, 117,* 103100. https://doi.org/10.1016/j.system.2023.103100.

Teng, L. S. (2022). *Self-regulated learning and second language writing: Fostering strategic language learners.* Cham: Springer.

Teng, L. S. (2024). Individual differences in self-regulated learning: Exploring the nexus of motivational beliefs, self-efficacy, and SRL strategies in EFL writing. *Language Teaching Research, 28*(2), 366–388. https://doi.org/10.1177/1362168821100688.

Teng, L. S., Yuan, E., & Sun, P. J. (2020). A mixed-methods approach to investigating motivational regulation strategies and writing proficiency in English as a foreign language contexts. *System, 88,* 102182. https://doi.org/10.1016/j.system.2019.102182.

Teng, L. S., & Zhang, L. J. (2016). A questionnaire-based validation of multidimensional models of self-Regulated learning strategies. *The Modern Language Journal, 100* (3), 674–701.

Teng, L. S., & Zhang, L. J. (2018). Effects of motivational regulation strategies on writing performance: a mediation model of self-regulated learning of writing in English as a second/foreign language. *Metacognition and Learning, 13*, 213–240. https://doi.org/10.1007/s11409-017-9171-4.

Teng, L. S. & Zhang, L. J. (2020). Empowering learners in the second/foreign language classroom: Can self-regulated learning strategies-based writing instruction make a difference? *Journal of Second Language Writing, 48*, 100701. https://doi.org/10.1016/j.jslw.2019.100701.

Teng, L. S. & Zhang, J. L. (2022). Can self-regulation be transferred to second/foreign language learning and teaching? Current status, controversies, and future directions. *Applied Linguistics, 43*(3), 587–595. https://doi.org/10.1093/applin/amab032.

Teng, M. F. (2016). Immediate and delayed effects of embedded metacognitive instruction on Chinese EFL students' English writing and regulation of cognition. *Thinking Skills & Creativity, 22*, 289–302. https://doi.org/10.1016/j.tsc.2016.06.005

Teng, M. F. (2019). A comparison of text structure and self-regulated strategy instruction for elementary school students' writing. *English Teaching: Practice and Critique, 18*(3), 281–297. https://doi.org/10.1108/ETPC-07-2018-0070

Teng, M. F. (2020a). The benefits of metacognitive reading strategy awareness instruction for young learners of English as a second language. *Literacy, 54*, 29–39. https://doi.org/10.1111/lit.12181.

Teng, M. F. (2020b). Tertiary-level students' English writing performance and metacognitive awareness: A group metacognitive support perspective. *Scandinavian Journal of Educational Research, 64*(4), 551–568. https://doi.org/10.1080/00313831.2019.1595712.

Teng, M. F. (2020c). Interactive-whiteboard-technology-supported collaborative writing: Writing achievement, metacognitive activities, and co-regulation patterns. *System, 97*, 102426. https://doi.org/10.1016/j.system.2020.102426.

Teng, M. F. (2020d). Young learners' reading and writing performance: Exploring collaborative modeling of text structure as an additional component of self-regulated strategy development. *Studies in Educational Evaluation, 65*, 100870. https://doi.org/10.1016/j.stueduc.2020.100870.

Teng, M. F. (2020e). The role of metacognitive knowledge and regulation in mediating university EFL learners' writing performance. *Innovation in*

Language Learning and Teaching, 14(5), 436–450. https://doi.org/10.1080/17501229.2019.1615493.

Teng, M. F. (2021a). The effectiveness of incorporating metacognitive prompts in collaborative writing on academic English writing skills. *Applied Cognitive Psychology, 35*(3), 659–673. https://doi.org/10.1002/acp.3789.

Teng, M. F. (2021b). Coupling text structure and self-regulated strategy instruction for ESL primary school students' writing outcomes. *Porta Linguarum, 31*, 61–76. https://doi.org/10.30827/portalin.v0i35.16861.

Teng, M. F. (2022a). Effects of cooperative–metacognitive instruction on EFL learners' writing and metacognitive awareness. *Asia Pacific Journal of Education, 42*(2), 179–195. https://doi.org/10.1080/02188791.2020.1835606.

Teng, M. F. (2022b). Effects of individual and group metacognitive prompts on tertiary-level students' metacognitive awareness and writing outcomes. *Asia-Pacific Education Researcher, 31*, 601–612. https://doi.org/10.1007/s40299-021-00611-8.

Teng, M. F. (2022c). Exploring awareness of metacognitive knowledge and acquisition of vocabulary knowledge in primary grades: A latent growth curve modelling approach. *Language Awareness, 31*(4), 470–494. https://doi.org/10.1080/09658416.2021.1972116.

Teng, M. F. (2023a). Metacognition. In Z. Wen, B., Adriana, B., Mailce, & F. Teng (eds.), *Cognitive individual differences in second language acquisition: Theory, assessment & pedagogy* (pp. 175–199). Berlin: De Gruyter Mounton.

Teng, M. F. (2023b). Exploring self-regulated vocabulary learning strategies, proficiency, working memory, and vocabulary learning through word-focused exercises. *The Language Learning Journal*. https://doi.org/10.1080/09571736.2023.2267575.

Teng, M. F. (2024a). Metacognition and autonomy in building a community for language learning through VR digital gaming. *Computers & Education: X Reality, 4*, 100060. https://doi.org/10.1016/j.cexr.2024.100060.

Teng, M. F. (2024b). Growth mindset in vocabulary learning from reading in a foreign language context. *International Journal of Applied Positive Psychology*. https://doi.org/10.1007/s41042-024-00161-6.

Teng, M. F. (2024c). Metacognitive awareness and EFL learners' perceptions and experiences in utilizing ChatGPT for writing feedback. *European Journal of Education, 60*, e12811. https://doi.org/10.1111/ejed.12811.

Teng, M. F. (2024d). Do self-efficacy belief and emotional adjustment matter for social support and anxiety in online English learning in the digital era?. *Digital Applied Linguistics, 1*, 2227. https://doi.org/10.29140/dal.v1.2227.

Teng, M. F., & Huang, J. (2019). Predictive effects of writing strategies for self-regulated learning on secondary school learners' EFL writing proficiency. *TESOL Quarterly, 53*, 232–247. https://doi.org/10.1002/tesq.462.

Teng, M. F., & Huang, J. (2023). The effects of incorporating metacognitive strategies instruction into collaborative writing on writing complexity, accuracy, and fluency. *Asia Pacific Journal of Education, 43*(4), 1071–1090. https://doi.org/10.1080/02188791.2021.1982675

Teng, M. F., & Ma, M. (2024). Assessing metacognition-based student feedback literacy for academic writing. *Assessing Writing.* https://doi.org/10.1016/j.asw.2024.100811

Teng, M. F., & Mizumoto, A. (2024). Validation of metacognitive knowledge in vocabulary. learning and its predictive effects on incidental vocabulary learning from reading. *International Review of Applied Linguistics in Language Teaching.* https://doi.org/10.1515/iral-2023-0294

Teng, M. F., Mizumoto, A., & Takeuchi, O. (2024). Understanding growth mindset, self-regulated vocabulary learning, and vocabulary knowledge. *System, 122*, 103255. https://doi.org/10.1016/j.system.2024.103255.

Teng, M. F. & Qin, C. (2024). Assessing metacognitive writing strategies and the predictive effects on multimedia writing. *Asia Pacific Journal of Education.* http://dx.doi.org/10.1080/02188791.2024.2325132.

Teng, M. F., Qin, C., & Wang, C. (2022). Validation of metacognitive academic writing strategies and the predictive effects on academic writing performance in a foreign language context. *Metacognition and Learning, 17*, 167–190. https://doi.org/10.1007/s11409-021-09278-4.

Teng, M. F., & Reynolds, B. L. (2019). Effects of individual and group metacognitive prompts on EFL reading comprehension and incidental vocabulary learning. *PloS ONE, 14*(5), e0215902. https://doi.org/10.1371/journal.pone.0215902.

Teng, M. F., Wang, C., & Zhang, L. J. (2022). Assessing self-regulatory writing strategies and their predictive effects on young EFL learners' writing performance. *Assessing Writing, 51*, 100573. https://doi.org/10.1016/j.asw.2021.100573.

Teng, M. F. & Yue, M. (2023). Metacognitive writing strategies, critical thinking skills, and academic writing performance: A structural equation modeling approach. *Metacognition and Learning, 18*, 237–260. https://doi.org/10.1007/s11409-022-09328-5.

Teng, M. F., & Zhang, D. (2024). Task-induced involvement load, vocabulary learning in a foreign language, and their association with metacognition. *Language Teaching Research, 28*(2), 531–555.

Teng, M. F., & Zhang, L. J. (2021). Development of children's metacognitive knowledge, reading, and writing in English as a foreign language: Evidence from longitudinal data using multilevel models. *British Journal of Educational Psychology*, *91*(4), 1202–1230.

Teng, M. F., & Zhang, L. J. (2022). Development of metacognitive knowledge and morphological awareness: A longitudinal study of ethnic minority multilingual young learners in China. *Journal of Multilingual and Multicultural Development*. https://doi.org/10.1080/01434632.2022.2052301.

Teng, M. F., & Zhang, L. J. (2024a). Ethnic minority multilingual young learners' longitudinal development of metacognitive knowledge and breadth of vocabulary knowledge. *Metacognition and Learning*, *19*, 123–146. https://doi.org/10.1007/s11409-023-09360-z.

Teng, M. F., & Zhang, L. J. (2024b). Assessing self-regulated writing strategies, working memory, L2 proficiency level, and multimedia writing performance. *Language Awareness*. https://doi.org/10.1080/09658416.2023.2300269.

Teng, M. F., & Zhang, L. J (2024c). Validating a new method for assessing young foreign language learners' metacognitive knowledge. *Research Methods in Applied Linguistics*, *3*(2), 100121. https://doi.org/10.1016/J.rmal.2024.100121.

Tseng, W.-T., Dörnyei, Z., & Schmitt, N. (2006). A new approach to assessing strategic learning: The case of self-regulation in vocabulary acquisition. *Applied Linguistics*, *27*, 78–102.

Urban, M., Urban, K., & Nietfeld, J. L. (2023). The effect of a distributed metacognitive strategy intervention on reading comprehension. *Metacognition and Learning*, *18*, 405–424.

Vandergrift, L. (2004). Listening to learn or learning to listen? *Annual Review of Applied Linguistics*, *24*, 3–25.

Vandergrift, L. (2005). Relationships among motivation orientations, metacognitive awareness and proficiency in L2 listening. *Applied Linguistics*, *26*, 70–89.

Vandergrift, L. (2007). Recent developments in second and foreign language listening comprehension research. *Language Teaching*, *40*, 191–210.

Vandergrift, L., & Baker, S. C. (2018). Learner variables important for success in L2 listening comprehension in French immersion classrooms. *Canadian Modern Language Review*, *74*, 79–100. https://doi.org/10.3138/cmlr.3906.

Vandergrift, L., & Goh, C. (2012). *Teaching and learning second language listening: Metacognition in action*. New York: Routledge.

Vandergrift, L., Goh, C., Mareschal, C. J., & Tafaghodtari, M. H. (2006). The metacognitive awareness listening questionnaire: Development and validation. *Language Learning*, *56*(3), 431–462.

Veenman, M. V. J., Van Hout-Wolters, B. H. A. A., & Afflerbach, P. (2006). Metacognition and learning: Conceptual and methodological considerations. *Metacognition and Learning*, *1*, 3–14.

Victori, M., & Lockhart, W. (1995). Enhancing metacognition in self-directed language learning. *System*, *23*(2), 223–234.

Weinert, F. E. (1987). Introduction and overview: Metacognition and motivation as determinants of effective learning and understanding. In F. E. Weinert & R. H. Kluwe (eds.), *Metacognition, motivation, and understanding* (pp. 1–16). Hillsdale, NJ: Lawrence Erlbaum.

Wen, Q., & Johnson, R. K. (1997). L2 learner variables and English achievement: A study of tertiary-level English majors in China. *Applied Linguistics*, *18*(1), 28–48.

Wen, Z., Sparks, R., Biedroń, A., & Teng, F. (2023). *Cognitive individual differences in second language acquisition: Theories, assessment and pedagogy*. Berlin: De Gruyter Mouton.

Wenden, A. L. (1987). Metacognition: An expanded view on the cognitive abilities of L2 learners. *Language Learning*, *37*(4), 573–597.

Wenden, A. L. (1998). Metacognitive knowledge and language learning. *Applied Linguistics*, *19*, 515–537.

Wenden, A. L. (2002). Learner development in language learning. *Applied Linguistics*, *23*, 32–55.

Winne, P. H., & Perry, N. E. (2005). Measuring self-regulated learning. In M. Boekaerts, P. R. Pintrich, & M. Zeidner (eds.), *Handbook of self-regulation* (pp. 531–566). Burlingtton: Elsevier Academic Press.

Zhang, L. J. (2001). Awareness in reading: EFL students' metacognitive knowledge of reading strategies in an acquisition-poor environment. *Language Awareness*, *10*(4), 268–288.

Zhang, L. J. & Zhang, D. (2018). Metacognition in TESOL: theory and practice. In J. I. Liontas (ed.), *The TESOL Encyclopedia of English Language Teaching*. Hoboken, NJ: John Wiley & Sons.

Zhang, L. J., Gu, Y., & Hu, G. (2008) A cognitive perspective on Singaporean primary school pupils' use of reading strategies in learning to read in English. *British Journal of Educational Psychology*, *78*, 245–271.

Zhou, S., & Rose, H. (2024). A longitudinal study on lecture listening difficulties and self-regulated learning strategies across different proficiency levels in EMI higher education. *Applied Linguistics Review*. https://doi.org/10.1515/applirev-2023-0113.

Zhou, S., Xu, J., & Thomas, N. (2024). L2 listening in a digital era: Developing and validating the mobile-assisted self-regulated listening strategy questionnaire (MSRLS-Q). *System, 123*, 103310. https://doi.org/10.1016/j.system.2024.103310.

Zimmerman, B. J. (2011). Motivational sources and outcomes of self-regulated learning and performance. In B. J. Zimmerman & D. H. Schunk (eds.), *Handbook of self-regulation of learning and performance* (pp. 49–64). Mahwah, NJ: Lawrence Erlbaum.

Zimmerman, B. J., & Bandura, A. (1994). Impact of self-regulatory influences on writing course attainment. *American Educational Research Journal, 31* (4), 845–862.

Cambridge Elements⁼

Language Teaching

Heath Rose
University of Oxford
Heath Rose is Professor of Applied Linguistics at the University of Oxford and Deputy Director (People) of the Department of Education. Before moving into academia, Heath worked as a language teacher in Australia and Japan in both school and university contexts. He is author of numerous books, such as *Introducing Global Englishes, The Japanese Writing System, Data Collection Research Methods in Applied Linguistics,* and *Global Englishes for Language Teaching*.

Jim McKinley
University College London
Jim McKinley is Professor of Applied Linguistics at IOE Faculty of Education and Society, University College London. He has taught in higher education in the UK, Japan, Australia, and Uganda, as well as US schools. His research targets implications of globalization for L2 writing, language education, and higher education studies, particularly the teaching-research nexus and English medium instruction. Jim is co-author and co-editor of several books on research methods in applied linguistics. He is an Editor-in-Chief of the journal System.

Advisory Board
Gary Barkhuizen, *University of Auckland*
Marta Gonzalez-Lloret, *University of Hawaii*
Li Wei, *UCL Institute of Education*
Victoria Murphy, *University of Oxford*
Brian Paltridge, *University of Sydney*
Diane Pecorari, *Leeds University*
Christa Van der Walt, *Stellenbosch University*
Yongyan Zheng, *Fudan University*

About the Series
This Elements series aims to close the gap between researchers and practitioners by allying research with language teaching practices, in its exploration of research informed teaching, and teaching-informed research. The series builds upon a rich history of pedagogical research in its exploration of new insights within the field of language teaching.

Cambridge Elements⁼

Language Teaching

Elements in the Series

Mediating Innovation through Language Teacher Education
Martin East

Teaching Young Multilingual Learners: Key Issues and New Insights
Luciana C. de Oliveira and Loren Jones

Teaching English as an International Language
Ali Fuad Selvi, Nicola Galloway and Heath Rose

Peer Assessment in Writing Instruction
Shulin Yu

Assessment for Language Teaching
Aek Phakiti and Constant Leung

Sociocultural Theory and Second Language Developmental Education
Matthew E. Poehner and James P. Lantolf

Language Learning beyond English: Learner Motivation in the Twenty-First Century
Ursula Lanvers

Extensive Reading
Jing Zhou

Core Concepts in English for Specific Purposes
Helen Basturkmen

Willingness to Communicate in a Second Language
Jian E. Peng

Teaching Second Language Academic Writing
Christine M. Tardy

Metacognition in Language Teaching
Mark Feng Teng

A full series listing is available at: www.cambridge.org/ELAT

For EU product safety concerns, contact us at Calle de José Abascal, 56–1°,
28003 Madrid, Spain or eugpsr@cambridge.org.

www.ingramcontent.com/pod-product-compliance
Lightning Source LLC
LaVergne TN
LVHW020350260326
834688LV00045B/1633